GHOSTS AND THE SUPERNATURAL

Pam Beasant

Illustrated by Tony Miller
and Richard Draper

Designed by Iain Ashman   Consultant Editor: Colin Wilson

Copy editor: Mike Halson   Picture Research: Constance Novis

CONTENTS

COLLINS

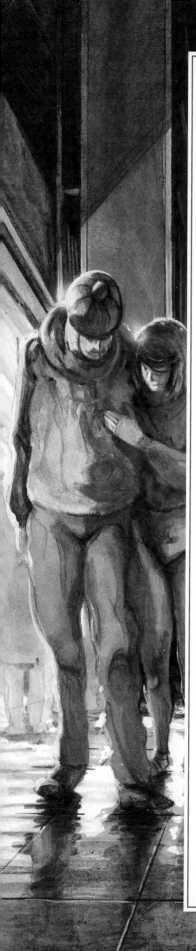

INTRODUCING GHOSTS

The world of ghosts is exciting and sometimes frightening. Although millions of people can claim to have seen a ghost, nobody yet knows what they are, where they come from, or why they haunt. Ghosts are hard to study as they always seem to appear when they are least expected, and are difficult to photograph or tape-record. What all ghosts have in common, however, is that they behave in a way that is 'beyond the natural world', or 'supernatural'. They can walk through solid objects, for example, or appear and disappear at will.

Different beliefs

Most people think that ghosts are the spirits, or *souls*,* of the dead. In some countries, such as China, it is believed that only people who were very evil or unhappy during life become ghosts. Others think that they are *devils* in disguise, or so-called 'nature spirits' of, for example, rocks and trees, who can take on human shape.

Some researchers think that ghosts may be like video recordings. For instance, if a person was very happy in a certain place, their feelings may have been strong enough to make an impression on the surroundings, like a photograph, which can be seen later on.

Ghosts with a purpose

Some ghosts seem able to see the future, and have appeared only once to give a warning of danger. Others have revealed buried treasure, and even unmasked a murderer. In 1681, an Englishman called James Graeme saw a blood-stained ghost  called Anne Walker. She said she had been murdered with a pickaxe on the orders of a relative. The man told the story to the magistrate and, after Anne's body was found, the relative and the murderer were both hanged.

Sometimes, ghosts of the living have appeared to a relative or friend, usually when the person whose ghost it is faces trouble or danger. This is called a *living ghost* (see page 8), or a wraith.

* Words in italics are explained in the Glossary on pages 46-47.

The ghost of a young Polish girl, who was killed in a car crash in 1931, in Chicago, USA, is said to jump into passing cars and tell the drivers she needs a lift home. When the cars reach Resurrection Cemetery on Archer's Avenue, Chicago, the ghost vanishes from the car and can be seen walking through the cemetery gates and then vanishing completely. The ghost has been nicknamed Resurrection Mary.

How ghosts look

Some ghosts look as solid as the living, until they suddenly vanish through a wall! Others may be a hazy outline, or are not visible at all but make their presence known by a sudden chill in a warm room or a swish of invisible petticoats. Many ghosts are totally unaware of people, or are so timid that they vanish if they are approached.

Ghostly animals and objects

It is not only people who return as ghosts. From all over the world there are stories of phantom animals, ranging from family pets to wild black leopards. In Europe, people used to be particularly afraid of animal ghosts because it was believed that animals had no souls, and therefore the *apparition* must be a devil in disguise. Some people, however, such as the North American Indians, have always believed in animals' spirits. After killing an animal they offered it food and treated it as an honoured guest, so that its spirit would not return for revenge. After this *ritual,* the animal could then be skinned and cooked.

Many reports of ghostly objects are of methods of transport, such as cars, trains and aeroplanes. In New York State, for example, the funeral train of Abraham Lincoln (who died in 1865) has been seen gliding along its old route, complete with a band of skeleton musicians on board.

Where to see a ghost

Ghosts can appear anywhere at all, from a modern bungalow to the middle of a wind-swept moor. There are some places, however, which are more likely than others to have ghosts, such as old buildings with a long history of people living and dying in them. Castles in particular tend to be haunted, perhaps because many people have suffered torture and cruel death in their dungeons.

Psychic powers

Some people seem to have minds that can easily 'tune in' to ghosts, like tuning in to a radio station. This ability is called *psychic* power, and although many people have it to a small degree, there are few who can control it. Those who can are often able to do other things as well, such as seeing into the future, or summoning spirits by going into a *trance.* Such people are called psychics or *mediums.*

Two brothers, driving along a lonely road in Scotland in 1962, came across a throng of ghosts which loomed out of the darkness from all sides. The most frightening moment came when a furniture van appeared so suddenly in front of them that the driver had no time to brake. As the car plunged into the back of the van, the van disappeared.

Some mediums claim to be able to contact spirits and make them appear. The photograph above is said to be of the ghost of a six-year-old girl called Rosalie, who was the child of one of the people present at the *seance.* Harry Price, a famous spirit investigator, was also there, and asked the ghost a number of questions before she vanished.

In 1870, an American cod-fishing schooner called 'Charles Haskell' accidentally rammed a sister-ship, the 'Andrew Johnson', which sank causing the death of all hands. The next Spring, when 'Charles Haskell' was back fishing, the lookouts witnessed a terrifying scene. A procession of 26 dead seamen climbed aboard the ship, went through the actions of sinking the fishing lines, then returned to the sea in silent procession.

Since 1971, in a house in a Spanish village, human faces have been appearing on a concrete floor. Baffled researchers have photographed and filmed the faces. They also covered the floor with tin foil for a month, and the faces continued to change.

RECORDINGS AND 'STAY-BEHINDS'

Some ghosts seem to be doomed forever to repeat the same actions over and over, as if they are either locked in a time warp, or are simply recordings like film characters. These ghosts are usually unaware of the living and are always seen or felt in the same place, sometimes over hundreds of years. An Australian researcher, Hans Holzer, called these ghosts 'psychic imprints'.

Two other kinds of ghost named by Holzer are 'stay-behinds' and 'true ghosts'. The 'stay-behinds' are the ghosts of people who, for various reasons, do not want to let go of their earthly lives, although they are aware that they are dead. 'True ghosts', says Holzer, are those which have not accepted, or recognized, that they are dead. They are stranded in this world, unable to function properly but with more power than 'psychic imprints'.

People who become 'true ghosts' are usually those who die suddenly, when the shock of the death somehow paralyzes the spirit so that it cannot move on. In 1915, for example, a young air mechanic called Freddy Jackson was killed instantly when he walked into an aeroplane propeller. Three days later, a group photo of the squadron was taken, and when it was developed, Freddy Jackson's face was clearly seen peering over the shoulder of a man in the top row – as if he did not realize he was dead.

Glamis Castle

Glamis Castle, in Scotland, is one of the most haunted and mysterious castles in the world. *Legends* tell of at least nine ghosts who seem bound to the castle because of their unhappy lives there. There is the woman with no tongue, who

Harry Martindale was working i a cellar in a house in York, England, in 1953. Suddenly, to his amazement, he heard the sound of a trumpet, and a Roman soldier came marching straight through the wall, followed by a whole column of soldiers, one of them on horse-back. The strange thing was that the soldiers' feet and the lower part of their legs wer

invisible until they reached a hole in the centre of the cellar, where they appeared complete as they walked through it.

Harry Martindale later found out that a Roman road ran under the house, at a lower level than the cellar floor. The hole, however, reached the surface of the old road, which is why the soldiers' legs could be fully seen as they marched through that part of the cellar.

peers from a barred window, or runs across the park, pointing at her mouth and screaming silently. There is also a little black boy, who is thought to have been a badly-treated servant – and Earl Beardie, who is said to have lost a card game with the Devil and can still be heard shouting and swearing. There is even supposed to be a restless female *vampire*! A blood stain, supposedly left by Malcolm II's murdered body, will not be scrubbed away – and two tall figures, one dressed in armour, enter bedrooms at night and frighten castle guests.

Re-runs

Sometimes living people experience frightening re-runs of past events in which they either watch, or take part in, whole scenes that happened many years before. It is as if the living go back in time and become ghosts in the past.

A young doctor in Wales was called out by a woman he did not know, called Jill. When he arrived, he found that he somehow knew all about her, and heard himself agreeing to help dispose of the body of her husband, whom Jill had just murdered.

Later, the doctor remembered that he had glanced in Jill's mirror and had been shocked to see, not his own face, but a stranger's. He hoped that it was all a nasty dream, but found out that Jill and the man in the mirror had really existed, and the events had happened just as he had experienced them, although many years before.

Ley lines

Some researchers believe that there are lines of magnetic force running through the earth, called *ley lines*. It is said that at certain points, such as where two or more ley lines cross, the force is particularly strong.

A researcher called T. C. Lethbridge (see page 31) noticed the force and thought that it may be electrical. He also believed it can record thoughts, feelings, images and sometimes whole scenes, and that people possess the power somehow to 'tune in' to this force and trigger a re-run of the things recorded. Lethbridge thought that most ghosts could be explained in terms of this force, and people's ability to tap it. It has since been noted that many hauntings do seem to occur on, or near, a ley line.

Ley lines are called dragon paths in China and Hong Kong, and fairy tracks in Ireland.

In Mannheim, West Germany, a man called Mr Lee was riding through a dark forest when suddenly he heard a horrible scream and saw a dark ragged figure running past him. He later found out that a mad woman had escaped from a nearby asylum 20 years before, and had been found in the forest with her throat cut. The screaming ghost had been heard and seen ever since.

In 1972, in Florida, USA, an Eastern Airlines Tristar jet crashed, killing 101 people. Since then, the dead pilot and flight engineer have been seen on the flight decks of other Tristars on more than 20 occasions.

One of the oldest ghost stories was told by the Ancient Roman writer Pliny the Younger. In a house in Athens, a hideous vision wrapped in ghostly chains appeared to the philosopher Athenodorus, and beckoned him into the garden. There, the bones of a man were found and were buried with the proper ceremonies. The mournful ghost was never seen again.

COMMUNICATING GHOSTS

Ghosts who bring messages to the living often attach themselves to one person, and can appear again and again until the message is acted upon. The message itself can be anything from a death warning to something quite trivial, such as a small unpaid debt. In 1838, a Scottish woman was troubled night after night by the ghost of a washer-woman who had left an unpaid grocery bill of three shillings and tenpence (about 19 new pence). Eventually, the grocer, who did not even know the woman was dead, was paid, and the ghost vanished forever.

In some cases, ghosts return to protect the living – such as the dead mother who uncovered a hidden document which gave financial security to her living children. Other ghosts want to put right their own wicked actions while alive. Nicolai Pomonareff, for instance, had had a long-standing quarrel with his son-in-law. After he died, Nicolai appeared and asked for his son-in-law's forgiveness, without which he could not rest. The son-in-law willingly shook the long, cold hand of the ghost, which was then at peace.

Unspoken messages

Sometimes ghosts do not communicate directly with the living, but make their feelings known in other, sometimes very unusual, ways. In 1965, in Virginia, USA, a woman inherited a portrait of a dead relative, Florence Wright. She was told that the portrait was beautifully coloured, so was surprised to find that, when she unwrapped it, it was in black and white.

Over the next few months, strange noises were heard in the room where the portrait hung. Then, to the owner's amazement, it began to take on colour until it was completely restored to its former self. A local *medium* said that Florence Wright's spirit was 'locked' inside the portrait, and had the power to drain it of colour, or restore it, depending on whether or not she was happy with the place where the portrait was hanging.

Warning ghosts

Ghosts seem to be able to see the future, and many have brought warnings of danger or death to the living. A story is told of a monk who was bricked up in his monastery long ago. His spirit is

In August 1974, a group of 30 young people, who were on the Japanese island of Okinawa for a folk concert, saw over a hundred female spirits in long white dresses moving on a large rock out at sea. The spirits appeared at night and were seen in the beam of a powerful torch. Apparently, the spirits are of people buried on the rock who have returned to show their disapproval of the modern age.

The American actor Telly Savalas ran out of petrol one night, and was thankful when a man in a black Cadillac offered him a lift. The next day, he rang the man to thank him again, but was told by the woman who answered that, although the man did seem to have been her husband, he had been dead for three years.

now said to wander in the countryside of Hampshire, England, where several people have seen him. Usually, he appears with his head turned away, but if he turns his face fully on a person, it is supposed to be a sign that they will shortly die.

In 1909, in London, England, a woman heard a clock in the hall strike 13; then, after a pause, it struck three more times. Three days later, the woman was killed in a taxi accident. Although there was no striking clock in the hall, the woman had heard the sounds before, shortly before her husband died. Again, the clock correctly predicted the number of days between the sounds and her husband's death.

Helpful ghosts

An actress who was living in France had been given a present of a painting by a friend. One night, the friend appeared to her, telling her to look behind the painting to find a present from the grave. She did so, and found an extremely valuable painting hidden behind the first. Later, she found out that her friend had died on the same day.

Another helpful ghost is that of a monk in St Andrews, Scotland, who appears on a steep flight of stairs in a church tower, and offers his help to those climbing the stairs, ensuring that they do not fall.

Fulfilling a promise

Some people, before they die, have promised to send a message from beyond the grave to someone they know. In Italy in 1905, two friends, Charles Galateri and M. Virgini, agreed that the one who died first would return and tickle the feet of the other. Six years later, Galateri's wife's feet were tickled. Looking around, she was horrified to see the ghost of a blood-stained Virgini, who waved cheerfully at her husband before vanishing. When they later discovered that Virgini had been killed, they realized he had been trying to fulfil his promise to Galateri.

Sometimes, a ghost appears because of a broken promise. Long ago, two Scottish women vowed that they would lay out the body of the one who died first – but when one died in childbirth, her friend was too busy to attend. Later that day, the corpse-like ghost of her angry friend appeared and sat in a chair by her fire, staring at her with accusing eyes.

An Italian man, Beniamino Sirchia, told Dr Caltagirone that he would return and break a hanging lamp above the doctor's table if he died first. Several months later, the lamp's cap was broken by a sharp, invisible blow. Sirchia had died soon before.

LIVING GHOSTS

Amazingly enough, there are more reported sightings of ghosts of people who are still alive than of those of the dead. These *'living ghosts'* are sometimes called 'crisis apparitions', as many of them appear at a time when the person whose ghost it is either faces great danger or is on the actual point of death.

Often, crisis apparitions appear to people they know, such as a member of their family, and they usually look perfectly solid and normal, sometimes even holding a conversation. In 1960, an American woman called Mrs Church, who was on holiday in India, woke up one night to hear her name being called by her brother, David. At the time, David was working in New York as an airline pilot, but when Mrs Church opened her eyes she saw him standing close to the bed dressed in his pilot's uniform. As she was about to speak to him, the figure melted away into nothing.

Later, Mrs Church discovered that David had had a near-accident in his aeroplane around the time she had seen him.

Telepathy

The ability to communicate by thought alone is called *telepathy* (see page 35). Many people believe that crisis apparitions are the result of a telepathy so intense that it can actually make the image of a person *materialize*. When Mrs Church's brother believed himself to be on the point of death, for example, his desire to tell his sister of his danger may have been so strong that he could somehow make his image appear to her to communicate his thoughts.

Doppelgängers

Some people have seen their own ghostly double. This strange kind of living ghost is usually called a *doppelgänger,* although in some countries it is called a fetch, or a judel.

Many believe that seeing your doppelgänger is a sign of death, although there are cases where they have not foreshadowed any disaster, and some where they even seem to have saved life. In 1944, for example, an American Army sergeant called Alex Griffiths was told to turn back by his doppelgänger as he led a patrol down a road in France. A few seconds later, a jeep which passed the patrol was attacked by a hidden machine gun.

For years, Ballachulish House, in the West of Scotland, was haunted by the ghost of a small woman. One day, a lady called Mrs Boulton visited the house, and told the owner, Lady Beresford, that she had often dreamed of the house before she had even heard of it. To her surprise, she was told that she was the 'ghost' that had often been seen wandering in the house.

In 1918, an English Royal Air Force pilot called David M'Connel was killed when his aeroplane crashed in fog during a short flight. Around the time of his death, his friend James Larkin was reading in his room at the RAF base. Suddenly, the door opened and David M'Connel walked in noisily, told Larkin that he had had a good trip, then left the room again, shouting goodbye. Later, James Larkin could hardly believe that M'Connel had been killed on his flight, and that he must have seen a ghost.

Twenty years later, Alex Griffiths was walking with his family through a wood in Canada. Again, his doppelgänger appeared and waved him back frantically. Just then, a tree fell right across the path with a huge crash. In both cases, the doppelgänger saved more than one life.

Mind-creatures

Some people, with highly developed powers of concentration through prayer or meditation, can actually produce 'ghosts' by thinking about them hard enough. Religious people in Tibet, called lamas, are especially good at this, and the forms they produce are called *tulpas* (some experts call them *elementals*).

A French woman called Alexandra David-Neel, who became a lama in Tibet, produced a tulpa in

the shape of a short, fat monk, who went everywhere with her and was seen by several people. When he began to get out of control, even taking on a rather nasty character, Alexandra David-Neel decided to try and 'dissolve' the tulpa, which she did only after six months of bitter struggle.

Out-of-the-body experiences.

Some researchers think that living ghosts are proof that part of the human mind, independently of the body, can somehow travel, communicate with others, and even produce solid-looking shapes. Although there are some who do not believe that this power exists, many have had experiences that suggest it is real.

The most common occurrences of this type are *out-of-the-body experiences,* in which people have claimed to have floated out of their bodies, and to have looked down on themselves from a distance. This has usually happened when the person has been unconscious, such as on the operating table, or as the result of an accident.

Some people have had the experience so regularly that researchers have been able to examine them scientifically. One woman was wired up to machines which measured her body movements and brain waves as she slept. On a shelf above the bed, which she could not reach without disconnecting the wires, a number had been placed which she was told to read while 'out-of-the-body'. She succeeded, and her brain waves recorded an unusual pattern at the time of her experience.

In 1771, the German poet Goethe saw his double riding towards him dressed in a grey suit trimmed with gold. Eight year later, when Goethe was riding along the same path, he realized with a shock that he was wearing the suit his double had worn, and must have seen his own future self on the earlier occasion.

POLTERGEISTS

Poltergeists are the most commonly-reported and the most strange and alarming of all 'ghosts'. The word poltergeist means 'noisy ghost' – a good description, as their behaviour is energetic, mischievous and sometimes frightening. For instance, a poltergeist can hurl objects around a room, or make heavy furniture move and sometimes disappear, only to reappear at once in another room. Pictures can fly off walls, and people have even been thrown out of bed by a strange force. In Lancashire, England, a cow was found stranded in a high hay-loft after a series of poltergeist activities on a farm. She could not have climbed the ladder herself, and had to be lowered using special equipment.

Everything about a poltergeist's activities suggests that there is a strong, controlling force behind them. Objects will cleverly avoid being caught in mid-flight, for example, and although they often land with great force, they are very rarely broken or damaged. They are, however, often too hot to touch afterwards.

Anything moved by a poltergeist also seems to defy all laws of space and gravity. An object may loop and twist in the air, for example, or squeeze through a space much smaller than itself. In one case, a block of wood flew between a man's fingers when the gap seemed impossibly small.

Very few people have been injured by a poltergeist. A vase, for example, may head straight for a person, then veer off at the last moment, or hit them with a light tap.

In some of the more alarming cases, strange voices have also been heard laughing, sobbing or screaming – sometimes they even foretell a future event, or scrawl messages across walls.

The phantom drummer of Tedworth

One of the most famous poltergeist cases began in 1661 in the small town of Ludgershall in East Wiltshire, England A visiting magistrate, John Mompesson, arrested a down-and-out, William Drury, when he refused to stop beating his drum and causing a disturbance. Drury escaped from prison and his drum was later sent to Mompesson's house in Tedworth for disposal.

After that, there was no rest for the Mompesson family – they heard violent raps and bangs all over the house, mingled with drum-beats. Every night,

On a rubber plantation in Sumatra in 1928, dinner guests took part in a strange event. A shower of pebbles suddenly landed on the veranda. The host then told the guests to mark the stones with chalk and throw them back to the bushes. Within a few seconds all but a few of the marked stones were 'thrown' back.

the racket went on for at least two hours and beds would be lifted off the floor. There was also a horrible smell. Over the next two years, the poltergeist slammed doors, rustled skirts and even jammed one of the horse's hooves into its mouth!

In 1663, William Drury was transported for theft. Before he went, he claimed to have caused the disturbances. Drury was known to have studied magic.

Different theories

Basically, no one knows what a poltergeist is. In the past, many hauntings now thought to be caused by poltergeists were believed to be the work of *devils,* or particularly malicious ghosts. Now, however, some researchers think that a poltergeist is not a ghost, but that somehow the human mind is capable of creating poltergeist activity. The ability to move objects through mind power is called *psychokinesis*, or PK for short.

Young people between the ages of 12 and 16 are often at the centre of poltergeist attacks, and it is thought that this age-group may be particularly able unknowingly to generate a burst of PK power which they cannot control. When PK is tested by scientists, however, the people who have the ability only seem to be able to move light objects, such as matchboxes, so the enormous amount of energy needed to move heavy furniture seems to be beyond the scope of ordinary PK.

Disproving a theory

Some poltergeist hauntings have been traced to quite ordinary causes. An earth tremor, for instance, which may not have been noticed, could cause houses to subside slightly, sometimes with terrifying creaks and bangs. Some people, therefore, believe that all cases of 'poltergeist activity' are due to such causes.

To test this idea, in 1961 a researcher called Tony Cornell borrowed a house which was due to be demolished, but was structurally sound. Using a vibrating machine and a huge 60-pound (27kg) weight, he sat inside the house while it was shaken and pounded by the machine and the weight. Even when the vibrations were strong enough to crack the house's structure, and send plaster cascading onto his head, none of the typical poltergeist signs were evident.

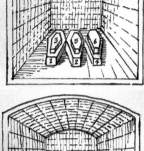

Was a poltergeist responsible for moving the coffins in a sealed family vault in Barbados? Between 1807 and 1820, every time the vault was opened to bring in another coffin the place was found in disarray. The coffins lay at all angles, and sometimes stood upright as if they had been flung across the chamber.

The Imperial Family of Russia was haunted by a ghost which appeared in the likeness of the person about to die. The Empress Catherine saw it sitting on her throne in 1796, and ordered the guards to shoot at it. It vanished, and Catherine died soon afterwards.

A Polish family is haunted by a yellowish-green ghostly face which appears in mirrors before a death. The ghost has never spoken, but there is an expression of demonic glee on its face every time it appears.

FAMILY GHOSTS

Many families have their own ghosts which stay with them, sometimes for hundreds of years. Often, a ghost attaches itself to the families of titled people, such as dukes and earls. This may be because, in the days when such families had enormous power over ordinary people, they sometimes committed terrible crimes which were never brought to justice. These dark secrets are the origin of the phrase 'a skeleton in the cupboard'.

The Scottish earls of Airlie, who live in Cortachy Castle, have been haunted by the ghost of a drummer boy. It is said that, long ago, one of the earls murdered the boy by throwing him from the castle tower inside his own drum. Before he died, the boy promised to haunt the family – and, ever since, a ghostly drum is heard before the death of every earl.

Not only rich and powerful families have their own ghosts. In Norway, for instance, a family has had ghostly warnings of death for many generations. Before the death, bedclothes appear as if someone is stretched out under them, or sometimes one of the pillows takes the shape of a nasty-looking face. In Denmark, a shopkeeper's family is haunted by the eerie appearance on a wall of the shadow of a gallows with a body hanging on it. It

appears before the death of a family member, and is said to have started 150 years ago, when an ancestor was wrongfully hanged for stealing.

Lights and shadows

Many European families, especially in Russia, Sweden and Wales, are haunted by strange lights called corpse candles which are a sign of a death in the family. Odd shadows which appear on walls or doors are also often regarded as ominous signs. Some more unusual family 'ghosts' have taken the form of swarms of gnats in Russia and grey pigs in Denmark.

Not all family ghosts are a sign of inevitable death. In Scotland, a branch of the Campbell clan was haunted by 'the green lady', who not only appeared sad at a family death, but also joyful if something good happened – and she enjoyed teasing the children as they lay in their beds.

The horrible hag of the dribble, whose appearance to Welsh families is a warning of death.

Fairies and banshees

A *banshee* is a kind of fairy (see page 19) who attaches herself to one family in Ireland (and sometimes Scotland), and wails at a time of death. She is very rarely seen but, in addition to her cries, she sometimes softly repeats the name of the one who will die.

In Northern Europe, most people used to believe in fairy spirits, and many still do. It is thought that sometimes one of them installs itself in a household and does the chores while the family sleeps. If fairy spirits are offended, however, they can cause havoc in the house, and disease in the family or in their animals.

The hag of the dribble

The hag of the dribble is a horrible sight with her black wings, long, tangled hair, hunchback and claws instead of fingers. She is a spirit that attaches herself only to Welsh families, and her name in Wales is Gwrach-y-rhibyn. Like a banshee, she appears only at the death of a family member, and makes a terrible noise – wailing and moaning, flapping her wings and tapping on windows with her claws. She has been seen at night occasionally, flying over country lanes and fields, making for the place where she will herald an approaching death.

About a hundred years ago, a hag of the dribble was frequently seen haunting the ruins of Pennard Castle in Wales. She was said to be looking for the family to which she was attached, unaware that they had died out of existence.

Although the hag of the dribble usually haunts old and powerful families, she appears to any who have pure Welsh blood.

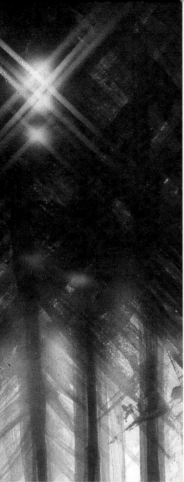

SUPERNATURAL LEGENDS AND BELIEFS

All round the world, the supernatural takes many different forms, ranging from a belief in animals which can turn into humans, to spirits which live in trees. The basis of all the beliefs, however, is the question of what happens to the human *soul* after death.

Souls

Most religions of the world agree that people have a soul which separates from the body at death. However, beliefs about what happens to the soul differ from country to country. In China, for example, it is thought that we have two souls. The first, called the superior soul, is good, and ghosts of this soul are not dangerous. But the second, called the inferior soul, associates with *demons* (see page 16) called kuei. It can re-animate corpses, and is dangerous to the living.

The land of ghosts

Many believe that there are special regions for the dead. For Jews and Christians, these are called heaven and hell, and the dead are sent to one or the other by God, depending on how they lived.

In British Columbia, Canada, the Tahltan Indians believe in a land of ghosts, where dead souls live like the living, but deep inside the earth. They can return to this life, but only as disembodied skulls which roll along the ground.

Many African tribes also believe in a realm of the dead which is hidden in the earth, and which the living have sometimes visited.

Rebirth

Buddhists think that souls are reborn in different forms, either animal or human, depending on what sort of life they have led. This is called *re-incarnation,* and it is believed that a soul, through several rebirths, can gradually work its way to Nirvana – a state of total happiness from which no rebirth is necessary. Japanese demons called gaki are believed to be the reborn souls of those who sinned during life, but not badly enough for their souls to be thrown into hell. One type of gaki lives

In the Pacific Islands, it is believed that the dead return as ghosts if they have failed to reach the spirit world. This might be because they have been attacked along the road by demons or other souls. Sometimes they appear in human shape, and sometimes in the form of animals or even fiery sparks. They are sad spirits which can be evil if they acquire special powers.

An old Russian story tells of a man who was attacked by a shrouded corpse on the way home from a day's hunting with his favourite dog. The dog flew at the corpse, and, as he grappled with him, the man ran for his life back home. Later, the dog was so furious about being abandoned that forever after he had to be chained up when his master appeared, as he would growl and bark as if he wanted to kill him.

in the 'World of Hungry Ghosts', and another type lives in this world, causing disease and death, and sometimes existing in the form of insects.

The walking dead

Many countries have stories about corpses that rise from their graves and terrorize people. This kind of ghost is one of the most horrible of all as it can feed on human blood. In some countries, they are called *vampires,* while in others they are believed to be demons who have taken over the dead body. (It is said Chinese vampires can even regenerate a body from a pile of bones.)

In Europe, it used to be thought that vampires were created by the Devil, and could be driven out through prayer and holy *exorcism.*

Some vampires take the form of animals, such as the Rumanian nosferat, who prowls at night in the shape of a cat, a dog, or a butterfly.

The demon vampire

A story is told in China of a man named Wang Fu, who was staying in the barn of an inn with three companions. The inn-keeper did not tell them that the body of his daughter-in-law lay behind a screen in the barn, waiting for burial. In the night, Wang Fu was horrified to see the corpse emerge from behind the screen, walk to his sleeping friends, pierce their necks and drink their blood. Wang Fu ran screaming from the barn, but the vampire followed. Eventually, he dodged behind a tree, causing the vampire to run straight into it.

The next day, the girl's body, abandoned by its demon, was found by locals – her claw-like nails were deeply embedded in the tree, and her dead eyes were fixed and staring.

The defeated corpse

A brave Russian man is said to have outwitted a vampire who had a taste for children. One day, as he walked past a graveyard, he was amazed to see a grave open and a corpse emerge who, after lay-ing aside its coffin lid, walked off towards the vil-lage. The man hid the lid and when the corpse returned, boasting that it had killed two children, he then said that he would keep the lid unless the corpse told him how to revive them. Reluctantly, it told him to cut off a piece of its shroud and put it in a pot with live coals. The smoke would waken the children. The man did this and the children revived. Later, angry villagers drove an aspen stake through its heart, and killed it forever.

In 1592, a German shoemaker killed himself by cutting his throat. Over the next few months, dozens of townspeople were reportedly terrorized by the man's ghost, which would attack people at night. When the corpse was dug up eight months later, it was apparently fresh and had even put on weight. When it was cut up and burnt, the ghost finally disappeared.

An old Japanese legend tells of a travelling priest who outwitted a horrible demon called a Rokuru-Kubi. By day, it appeared to be a normal person, but at night, its head left its body and flitted about causing mischief. The priest knew that if the body were to be moved while the head was away, then the demon would die. He did this and the demon died after lunging its head at him and fastening its teeth onto his sleeve.

All Hallows' Eve, or Hallowe'en, used to be an important festival for the dead. Bonfires were lit on hilltops to keep away evil spirits and witches. Nowadays, Hallowe'en is more of an excuse to dress up and go round the neighbours collecting fruit, sweets or money. The question 'trick or treat?', asked by American children, means that if they are not given a treat, they will play a trick in the manner of the supernatural beings they resemble.

EVIL SPIRITS

In most countries, people have always believed in a mixture of supernatural forces. Spirits called *demons,* for instance, represent a force of evil. Their purpose is always to harm people, and they achieve this in various ways. Some demons are said to be able to attack people directly, while others resort to trickery and pranks. In many countries, demons are held responsible for a whole range of things from insect bites to death.

In Siberia, a story is told of how, long ago, a demon-monster called Adalma-Muus terrorized people by rising from the bottom of the sea, seizing them with his long tongue and taking them back to his watery den to devour them. One day, however, a good spirit called Tyurun Nuzykay grabbed the demon's tongue and held it while he drank all the water until it reached the demon's ankles. Then he pulled the demon onto land and beat him to death. The remains of the monster were said to turn into biting insects which flew away and plague the world to this day.

Similarly, a Japanese legend tells how the remains of demons can be found in the form of worms, ants, beetles, scorpions, snails and centipedes.

Some demons are not wholly bad. Although the Indian rakshasas are horrible looking, with long slit eyes and deformed bodies, they occasionally take a liking to a person and help them with their lives, usually making them very rich.

Why do demons exist?

In some countries, it is believed that demons were once humans who were so wicked that their *souls* became supernaturally evil. Another belief is that they are unhappy spirits who are, for various reasons, earthbound. Other demons are said always to have been spirits, who existed before people. Some religions teach that demons are there so that people can see and understand wickedness and turn away from it to good. Many people, however, believe that demons do not exist at all, or are just an invented symbol of evil.

Jinns

Jinns are strange creatures which are said to be like demons, but mortal. They can change their shape at will, and often cause mischief to people. They live in drains, wells, cemeteries, and even in houses. It is thought that genies (such as the one in Aladdin's lamp) and ghouls are both types of jinns.

A young Russian blacksmith once had a painting of a demon which he hated, and every morning would spit at it. The demon decided to play a trick. He changed himself into a young man and became the blacksmith's apprentice. One day, while he was alone, he transformed an old countess

Familiars

In the 17th century, many women were killed on suspicion of being a *witch*. This meant that people believed that they had sold their souls to the Devil and could perform *black magic* (see page 23) to harm people. Witches were also thought to have *familiars,* which were demons assigned to them by the Devil to keep an eye on them and help them with their *spells*. The familiars could take the shape of just about anything, but were said to be usually dogs, cats, toads or goats.

Fear of witches was so strong that thousands of women in Europe and America died who are now thought to have been completely innocent.

Combating evil spirits

It is widely believed that all forces of evil are balanced by forces of good which are represented by good spirits. Sometimes they are called *angels* and their purpose in the world is always to do good and help people, and protect them against evil. The Maori people of New Zealand, for instance, believe that gods and goddesses called atuas protect them, and each family has its own atua which can be called in time of need through the priests (called tohungas).

According to the Chinese, good spirits are beautiful, and in some cases have even married humans. In many countries, people believe that the spirits of their dead ancestors watch over them. If treated with proper respect, the ancestors will help their living family, but if they are neglected they can cause terrible misfortunes.

Possession and exorcism

Some people think that demons can enter a person's body and 'take them over', making them say and do terrible things. This is called *possession*. Usually, a holy person, such as a priest, can make the demon leave by praying with the person and carrying out a *ritual* known as *exorcism*. The demon is generally unwilling to go, and exorcism is often a long, painful, and sometimes dangerous process for all concerned.

Many doctors and scientists now believe that possession is not due to a demon, but to medical conditions such as epilepsy or hysteria, both of which can cause convulsions of the body and foaming at the mouth – two things which used to be taken as signs of possession.

into a young woman. When the count appeared wanting the same treatment, the blacksmith did not know how to do it, and the countess ordered him to be hanged. At last the demon reappeared and changed the count, and the blacksmith showed him more respect.

North American Indians used to believe that in order to reach full maturity each had to make contact with a personal *guardian spirit* (see page 21) who would protect them always. This was done when the spirit revealed itself and taught the Indian a spirit song, which, when sung, would call up the spirit at any time. Each song was a closely guarded secret, known only to the one to whom it had been taught.

In some countries, death itself has been thought of as a demon or creature. It has acquired many different names in different countries. In Brittany, France, for instance, it used to be called Ankou, and looked like a skeleton. Another European name for death was the Wild Huntsman, as he was thought to ride through the skies leading a multitude of demons.

A 12th-century writer called Giraldus Cambrensis wrote about a werewolf *curse* put upon the inhabitants of the region of Ossary in Ireland in the 6th century. Every seven years, two people from the region had to become wolves. If they survived, they were allowed to return to their old lives, and two more had to take their places. The curse was put upon the people by an abbot, as punishment for wicked behaviour.

The Japanese have always been superstitious about foxes, believing them to have the power to turn into beautiful women, and cause trouble to people. During the Second World War, the Americans experimented with breeding glowing foxes. They were going to set them loose in Japan before a planned invasion, and so weaken the morale of the people. The project, however, was cancelled when the war ended.

LEGENDARY CREATURES

The belief in creatures such as werewolves, nature spirits and fairies is very ancient. Although they are now often regarded as myths rather than real, there are still those who claim to have come across them. In Ireland, for instance, there is a healthy respect for fairies, and few Chinese would scoff at the idea of *werebeasts*.

Werebeasts

Werebeasts can change their shape at will from human to animal. They occur in various forms, the most common and best known being werewolves.

Those who believe in werebeasts say that they are either evil spirits, people suffering from a magic *curse,* or magicians magically disguising themselves. Werefoxes in China, however, are slightly different, as they are basically ordinary foxes with the power to turn into a woman. They are also different because they are not completely evil. Sometimes they even marry humans. The Japanese also believe in werefoxes (or fox-maidens), but this time they are evil and dangerous.

In Africa, there is a belief in were-hyenas, which, like fox-maidens, are basically animals who can change their shape. One old story tells of a young woman who fell in love with a visiting stranger. She married him and they set off for his native village. Suspecting something evil about the man, however, her brother followed the couple to the village. That night, as he hid, the brother saw that the village men had turned into hyenas and were discussing how they would eat his sister when she was fat. The next day, the brother carved a magic wooden bowl, into which he and his sister climbed and were carried safely back to their village.

Elementals

A 16th-century man known as Paracelsus wrote down most of what we know about spirits called *elementals.* Elementals are nature-spirits who are associated with the four elements – air, water, earth and fire. The elementals of the air are called sylphs, those of the water are nymphs, or undines, those of earth are gnomes, and those of fire are called salamanders or vulcans. These four kinds of spirit are made of flesh and blood like humans, but they have no *soul* and can move about as

A modern *occult* writer, Dion Fortune, claims to have *'materialized'* a sort of werewolf, or elemental. She was lying in bed feeling angry with an acquaintance. Half asleep, her thoughts turned to an old wolf legend. Suddenly, she felt a movement in her solar plexus, and saw a wolf standing by the bed. It lay down beside her and she could feel the weight of its

quickly as 'pure' spirits. It is now believed that Paracelsus made up most of the details about elementals, although he did draw on *legends* and *superstitions* from many countries.

In the past, belief in elementals was much more general. It was thought that everything – trees, flowers, rivers, fields, hills and clouds – had its own spirit. This belief was called *animism*, from the Latin word animus, which means 'life', 'soul,' or 'spirit'. The North American Indians are animists – they believe that animals and all natural things have a soul or spirit equal to that of people.

Fairies

Fairies are said to live all over the countryside and sometimes in people's houses. From country to country, their names and characters vary, but they are almost always mischievous and sometimes dangerous to humans. Belief in fairies used to be widespread all over Europe, but there are now fewer believers although some remain, especially in Britain, Ireland, Scandinavia and Iceland.

There are an enormous variety of fairies. Brownies and lobs, for instance, are household spirits, attached to one family, who sweep and clean at night in exchange for small gifts of money or food. Irish leprechauns are tiny shoemakers who have hordes of gold for which mortals long. Some fairies are also believed to be guardians of animals, plants or crops and are thought of as similar to elementals.

Some fairies are terribly evil and dangerous, such as the Scottish redcaps, who are said to have murdered travellers and dipped their caps in the blood. Glaistigs are also evil. They appear as beautiful women but suck the blood of any mortal man who dances with them. Water kelpies take the shape of horses and lure people into water on their backs to eat them.

Fairies can be anything from 15 centimetres to 250 centimetres tall. Some are very beautiful, while others are wrinkled and deformed. Like humans, they need food, drink and sleep – one kind of fairy was known to creep into houses at night and roast frogs in front of the fire.

No one has ever been sure what fairies are. Some think they are ghosts of the dead, or *demons*, while others think they are creatures half-way between humans and *angels*. It is also thought by some that *poltergeist* activity in the past was blamed on fairies and that is how fairy legends began.

body against her legs. The next night, she saw the wolf again, and concentrated on drawing it back inside herself. It slowly vanished.

Dion Fortune believes that the wolf was the product of her own mind, although it was visible to others – rather like the tulpas materialized by the lamas of Tibet (see page 9).

Kobolds are small, troublesome fairies who live in mines in Germany. They often disturb the miners and undo jobs that have just been done. Sometimes, however, they do help with the work if they are in the mood.

These pictures were taken in the 1930s by a 15-year-old girl called Elsie Wright in Yorkshire, England. They were thought at the time to prove that fairies really existed, but the photographs are now believed to have been faked – the 'fairies' being cardboard cut-outs from a magazine.

The people of the South Pacific Islands believe in the magical and protective power of jade. Talismans in the shape of a human figure are carved from jade, and often worn around the neck to protect the wearer from evil. The Chinese also believe that jade has special power and sometimes bodies are buried with almond-shaped jade discs over the eyes.

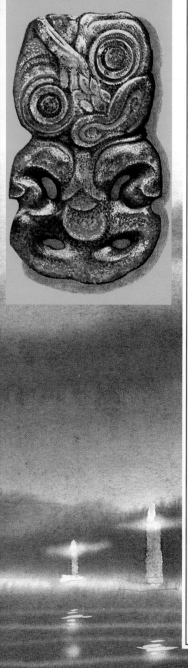

DEFENCES AGAINST GHOSTS

There are many things that people do to ensure that the spirits of the dead rest in peace and do not come back as ghosts to trouble them. There are also defences against all kinds of evil spirits, *vampires* and *witches*. Sometimes, these *rituals* are so old that their original purpose has been forgotten and they have become vague *superstitions*. Throwing spilled salt over the left shoulder, for instance, used to be protection against the Devil, as the salt was said to land in his face.

Funeral rites

The most important defences against ghosts in many countries are the *funeral rites* carried out when someone dies. These rituals often commence before the funeral begins. One old belief was that if a person died at home, all mirrors must be covered up, as the *soul* might grab the reflection of a living person and take it away to the after-life.

The Kamchadale people of North-East Asia believed that death tainted a house, and would abandon any place where a death occurred.

In Northern Europe, mysterious letters called runes used to be carved inside tombs to keep away evil, and to prevent the corpse leaving the grave. Some runes spelled out *curses* to those who might disturb the grave. Runes were thought to have magic power.

The bushmen of South Africa believe that death is not natural – that a person dies because evil spirits have entered them and taken them away, or caused disease. Because of this, they have a particular fear of ghosts, and weigh down a corpse with heavy stones to prevent it returning.

The Eskimos remove corpses from houses through a window or the smoke-hole, as it is thought that if they are taken through the door, then the spirit will find its way back to the house. Sometimes traps are placed at the house door as a further prevention. During mourning, the living will not utter the name of the dead person and do not use any sharp tools in case they injure the ghost and make it angry. As in many countries, the corpse is buried with water, food, weapons and tools for use in the spirit world. Eskimos also hold several feasts in honour of the dead, during which they invite the dead back to this world to be nourished by their descendants.

An event called Obon is held in Japan each year. Candles are lit for the dead and special meals prepared. On the 15th August, a Buddhist priest reads out the names of the dead from pieces of paper which are then taken by the relatives and floated down a river, to send the spirits back to the spirit world.

At Chinese funerals, drums are beaten and fireworks set off to frighten evil spirits away. Paper models of cars, houses and money are also burnt as these are believed to help the soul pay its way through the ten courts of judgement in the afterlife.

Charms

One of the most effective *charms* is garlic, which is thought to ward off witches, vampires and all evil spirits. Sometimes, wreaths of garlic flowers are placed on graves. Silver and cold iron are also said to be protective.

According to tradition, a vampire could be killed by a silver bullet, and any evil thing fears iron. Because of this, iron was often placed in coffins, or at the threshold of houses where a death had occurred.

In many countries, it used to be believed that bats had magical power. In some they were evil, while in others they were lucky. The people of Hessen in Germany believed that a bat's heart attached to a gambler's arm would bring success at cards. In parts of Austria, it was said that a bat's eye could make a person invisible.

The Ancient Roman writer Pliny recommended that a hyena's tooth be worn around the neck for protection against ghosts. He also said that blood from a hyena smeared round the door will block a wizard's magic power. The Chinese believe that burning a joss-stick will keep away evil spirits and please the gods.

Guardian spirits

Often, *guardian spirits* are those of ancestors, but they can also be other kinds of spirits which attach themselves to one person or family, or act as guardians for a whole community, or a sacred place such as a church or a graveyard. At a temple in Bangkok, for instance, the figure of a Dutch sea captain is said to keep away evil from the temple.

An old European tradition was that the first person to be buried in a graveyard became its guardian forever and protected the other dead. Houses were also protected by a guardian spirit, and sometimes a corpse was even buried at the threshold for this purpose.

Mohammedans believe that each man has four guardian spirits – two for the night and two for the day. At sunrise and sunset, they change guard, and it is then that the man is most likely to be invaded by *demons*. The Kalanga tribe of Botswana, Africa, believe in protective demons called mazenge. Through women *mediums,* they relay messages and medicines to the people, while the mediums dance in a *trance* throughout the *ritual.*

In Eastern countries, kite-flying forms part of many rituals to ward off spirits. The kites are often in the shape of animals and birds – and sometimes dragons.

A ghostly child called Malekin was the guardian spirit of a house in England long ago. He was said to be very sociable and clever and could discuss the Bible in fluent Latin.

MAGIC

Magic is based on the belief that there is a strong force running through nature and all living things, and that people can tap this force and make it do anything they want, from enabling hunters to catch food to causing thunderstorms. In tribal communities, this force is called mana and it is used by *witches* and *witch doctors* (or 'nganga'). Mana is brought into force by calling up spirits, and those who perform magic think that the spirits are essential to make it work. Witch doctors call on spirits of ancestors to help them find the cure to an illness, or to find a thief in the tribe.

In order to perform magic, it is essential to get into the right state of mind, and concentrate your whole will on what you are trying to do. For this reason, witch doctors will often go into a *trance* by dancing and singing in a frenzy until they believe that their guiding spirit has taken possession of them and they are ready to perform magic.

Shamans

Every tribal society has holy men and women who, like African witch doctors, act as *mediums* between the people, the spirit world and the forces of nature. These people are called *shamans* and they have strong mental and *psychic* powers. In most tribes, the 'call' to be a shaman runs in families and may take the form of a dream, or a serious illness from which a person will only recover if they accept their call to shamanism. Like witch doctors, shamans spend most of their time healing, or appealing to the spirits for good hunting and healthy children for the tribe. Some, however, use their powers for evil purposes.

In order to contact the spirits, a shaman will usually go into a trance, sometimes by beating a drum which is thought to have magic powers.

Why magic is used

For most tribes, magic is a vital part of life as it is seen to give people control over their surroundings, so that they feel less vulnerable to sudden illnesses or disasters.

In hot, dry regions such as Africa most tribes believe that the right magic will bring rain to help food grow. Appealing to the rain god is one of the witch doctor's most important functions, as a bad harvest due to dry weather can mean the difference between life and death. The whole tribe is

Malicious people who try to injure, and sometimes kill, others through magic often use as part of the ritual a doll or other human image. They 'injure' the doll in the same way that they want the real person to be injured – acting out the damage in advance. This is called *imitative magic*. It is not always bad, as it is sometimes used to heal people, and some tribes use it to ensure good hunting or healthy children.

Tribal shamans, who are both priests and magicians, have to go through rigorous initiation rites before they can begin practising. These vary from country to country – Eskimo shamans, for instance, have to endure five days in freezing water. The rituals are designed to test the shaman's power of will to resist pain, and to shock their minds into a fully alert state.

Those who practise magic often claim to be able to summon up *'apparitions'* of *demons,* spirits and even animals. One witness to an African ceremony, Harry Wright, described how a young girl danced a 'leopard dance' by firelight. As she danced, Wright could see shadows all around her which his companion said were clearly leopards. At the high point of the dance, three real leopards suddenly appeared, walked across the clearing and disappeared back into the jungle. It was as if they had come to investigate the phantom leopards called up by the dance.

involved in the rain-making ceremony. They sing, dance and pray while the witch doctor works himself into a frenzy to appeal to the rain god.

Other important functions of the witch doctor are to ensure successful food hunting, find criminals within the tribe, and cure illness.

Good and bad magic

Many tribes think that most illnesses and general misfortunes are caused by evil magic, called *black magic,* which is performed by bad witches. Bad witches might be people who have turned from good magic to bad, or the evil might be in the family. It is the witch doctor's job to find, by various methods, who the bad witch is.

Some methods of finding bad witches use special equipment, such as divining bones, or testing a hen's reaction to poison – if the hen dies, it is a sign of guilt. Sometimes the accused is given poison, and the degree of illness that results indicates guilt or innocence.

Voodoo

Voodoo is a religious cult that originated in Dahomey, Africa, but is now practised mainly in the Caribbean island of Haiti, and by black Americans in the Deep South (where it is called Hoodoo). The main purpose of voodoo is for the individual worshipper to make contact with the supernatural world of spirits, including various gods and goddesses, and the *souls* of the dead. At a voodoo ceremony, the people become 'possessed' by a spirit while in a trance. Through the priests and priestesses (called hungans and mambos), appeals are made to the spirits who rule all aspects of life.

Hexing and bone-pointing

In most tribes all over the world, the effects of a magical *curse* (also called hex or malediction) are immediate and deadly. In Australia, for instance, a method of executing criminals amongst the Aborigines is 'bone-pointing'. A piece of bone, sharp at one end and with a lump of gum containing human hair at the other, is pointed at the victim after certain *rituals* have been observed. Usually, the victim falls ill at once, and dies within hours or days. It is thought that these methods work because people believe in them strongly – victims fully believe they are doomed and the fear and shock can bring about actual death.

For years there have been reports that *zombies* (the 'walking dead') have been seen working as slaves in Haiti. One man, Clairvius Narcisse, claims that he himself was a zombie. He says that in 1962 a voodoo priest drugged him so that it appeared that he was dead, then dug him up after his funeral and took him away as a slave, still drugged. Two years later, Narcisse regained his memory and escaped. In 1980, he returned to his native village to the astonishment of those who had mourned his death.

This engraving shows the 16th-century astrologer and magician John Dee, standing inside a magic circle with his assistant, Edward Kelly, having called up a spirit. The circle, still used by magicians and witches, protects against spirits which have been called up, and helps concentrate the energy needed for the process inside a confined space.

In 1666, the Dutch physician Helvetius was shown some lumps of stone by a stranger and told that they were 'the philosopher's stone' – the secret of eternal life – and they could change lead into gold. Helvetius stole a grain, but when he tried it, the lead exploded. The next day the man came back with more of the stone, and this time Helvetius is said to have made gold.

USES OF MAGIC

Many magicians nowadays are entertainers who perform tricks that look like magic. No real magic is involved and no stage magicians claim to have real magic power. There are still some 'real' magicians, however, carrying on an ancient tradition based on the idea that there is a power running through everyone and everything that can be tapped and controlled through calling up spirits.

The secrets of this power have evolved over thousands of years – some are written down in special books which are studied by magicians.

Alchemy

In the 17th century, many of those interested in magic explored it through studying *alchemy*. The aim of alchemy was to attempt to change ordinary metals, such as lead and mercury, into gold. The belief that this could be done was based on the old law of magic – 'as above, so below', which implies that people can achieve anything through the power of the will. Alchemists also searched for the ultimate power – the philosopher's stone – which was the secret of eternal life.

Alchemy was thought of as the ultimate test of a magician's power. Many tried for years to produce gold, but as the process was kept secret, it is not now clear how, or if, it was done. Even those who knew what chemicals to use, and in what proportions, often failed because they could not find that extra ingredient which seems to have been an enormous burst of concentrated will-power from the alchemist.

One Englishman called James Price claimed to have found the secret in 1782 and invited a group of men to watch as he added a red powder to mercury and produced gold. Asked to prepare more powder, however, he said that it was too damaging to his health. When the group pressed him, Price became so desperate that he took poison in front of them. If he had found the alchemists' dangerous secret, then it died with him there.

Healing magic

Magic has always been used for healing. Like tribal *shamans* and *witch doctors,* there are those who claim to diagnose and cure illness through *psychic* power. In the 1920s, a French woman called Celine could 'see' inside of the body like a human X-ray machine, and diagnose illness from that.

In the 17th century, the traditional view of witches was that they flew about on broomsticks and pitchforks and danced with *devils* at the witches' sabbath. During the witchcraft trials, some people claimed to use 'flying ointment' to enable them to do this. It was found, however, that the ointment, made mainly from poisonous plants and ingredients such as bats' blood, induced a drugged state which made people believe they were flying, when they were really lying senseless on the floor.

This is called *autoscopy*. Some healers use religious faith as the source of their power, and this is called faith healing.

Particular cures and *spells* are sometimes used for minor illnesses. In Cornwall, England, there are 'wart-charmers' who cure wart-sufferers in a number of ways. Some 'buy' the warts, paying a few pence for each. Others rub a piece of bacon on them, which must then be buried.

Modern witchcraft

Modern *witches* are men and women who practise *rituals* which, they claim, are based on an ancient religion which worshipped the forces of nature in order to ensure the earth's fertility. Unlike some magicians, they do not attempt to dominate these forces for personal power, but simply recognize them as part of their religion (which is sometimes called *wicca*).

Although modern witches are often regarded with suspicion, they emphasize that any magic they perform is for good purposes such as healing. They believe that bad spells will rebound threefold on their heads. Each group of witches has a high priestess, who represents the main goddess of the religion and wears her symbols of the moon and the stars in the form of a crescent headdress. There is also a high priest who represents the goddess's consort (partner) in heaven.

The witchcraft trials

In the 15th to 17th centuries, thousands of people were executed in Europe and America for being witches. It was thought that they had sold their souls to the Devil, and had been given evil powers. Witches were supposed to be able to change their shape, ride through the air to the witches' sabbath (a meeting of witches), and, through spells, do anything from blasting crops to causing illness.

Witches were also believed by some to have a place on their bodies where they could not feel pain (called the 'mark of the witch'), and many were subjected to painful searches for this mark. Other beliefs were that witches would float when thrown, tied up, into ponds.

Often, people accused of witchcraft were forced to confess after torture, and if they did so, their families were likely to be suspected also. Most of those accused were burnt – sometimes the victims were mercifully strangled first so that they did not feel the flames.

Aleister Crowley, the most notorious magician this century, was born in 1875. Nicknamed 'The wickedest man in the world', and calling himself 'The Beast', Crowley used his reportedly genuine magic powers for his own ends. On one occasion, on being asked to demonstrate his powers while walking down a street in New York, Crowley fell into step behind a man. Suddenly, Crowley buckled his legs and sat down for a second on his haunches. The man's legs also buckled and he fell to the ground in complete surprise.

The main equipment of modern magicians are the sword, the wand, the chalice and the pentacle. The sword is used for protection against any *demons* who may appear, while the chalice represents water and the ideas of love and fertility. The wand helps the magician conjure his magic, and the pentacle represents the earth – it is a flat circle with magical symbols drawn on it. The magician often uses incense and perfumes during rituals.

In a typical seance, people sit in a circle, and touch hands to help concentration (and to make sure that no one cheats!). The medium then goes into a trance and the spirits might show their presence by moving the table. Sometimes the lights are dimmed and music is played.

PSYCHIC POWERS

People who are sensitive to supernatural forces are called *psychics* and are said to have psychic powers. These can take many forms, ranging from moving objects through mind power to predicting the future. Traditionally, however, those who displayed psychic powers became *mediums*.

Mediums

Mediums claim to be able to communicate at will with the spirits of the dead. This usually happens at a meeting called a *seance*, where the medium goes into a *trance*, makes contact with the spirit world and brings messages from it to the people in the group (the 'sitters'). Some mediums use *'controls'*, which are spirits who act as guides in the spirit world and through which the medium often receives messages from other spirits.

In some countries, mediums have always been an important part of life. African *witch doctors* (or 'nganga') are mediums, and use their psychic power mainly for healing purposes. Guided by the spirit of a dead relative, the witch doctor often finds the solution to problems and cures illnesses through herbal remedies.

Spiritualism

The belief that the spirit of a person survives death and can be contacted in the spirit world has been commonly held for a long time. In 1848, however, this belief became a movement called *spiritualism,* with professional mediums, after two American sisters, Margarette and Kate Fox, claimed that the spirits spoke to them in a code of raps and bangs. Soon millions of people in America and Europe were holding seances, and devices were even developed to receive the spirits' messages. A *ouija board,* for instance, contains the letters of the alphabet and spells out messages, guided by 'the spirits'. A planchette, which is a pencil mounted on wheels, would sometimes be used on a ouija board.

'Physical' mediums

At the beginning of this century, a large number of 'physical' mediums were discovered, through which the spirits seemed to produce amazing effects during seances. Some, for instance, *levitated* (rose unaided from the ground). Others

Daniel Dunglas Home, a Scottish-born American, was a spectacular medium who conducted hundreds of seances in the last century. He could levitate, make his body longer, or touch burning coals without pain. At one seance, he stuck his head right into a burning fire. At another, he reportedly floated out of a window and back in through another. Rapping noises and invisible pinching fingers were also regular features of Home's seances.

caused objects to move, glowing lights to appear, or musical instruments to play by themselves. Some even seemed to produce strange disembodied hands or feet, called *pseudopods*, which would pinch, stroke or prod the sitters at the seance.

Occasionally, physical mediums would produce a white substance called *ectoplasm* which oozed from their bodies, and from which faces or even whole people would emerge. For example, an Algerian medium called Marthe Beraud produced ectoplasm which came out at first like steam, before gradually taking shape. Many people said that the ectoplasm was really material such as muslin or gauze on which she had already drawn the faces or limbs. Eye-witnesses, however, claimed that this was impossible.

'Mental' mediums

Most mediums today are 'mental' mediums who confine their activities to bringing messages from the dead. Some prefer to do this with just one sitter at a time, while others hold large public meetings where many spirits speak to various members of the audience. Usually, a wide range of messages are received, from simple reassurances that a spirit is happy, to very detailed disapproval of something a living relative may be doing.

One of the most successful mental mediums this century was Mrs Osborne Leonard, who held hundreds of seances in the 1920s, speaking through her control, 'Feda', while in a trance. To prove that she really existed, Feda would correctly predict future newspaper articles, or tell sitters exactly what was written on a certain page of a book in their library.

Different theories about mediums

Some researchers say that mediums use unconscious *telepathy,* reading the minds of their sitters for their information. Often, however, facts emerge which are unknown to the sitter at the time. A dead soldier, for instance, told his cousin at a seance to give his pearl tie-pin to his fiancée. The cousin did not know that the fiancée existed, but she was eventually found.

Some mediums, while in a trance, speak in languages they do not know. It is thought that they may, at some point in the past, have seen the language written, and unconsciously remembered it. No theory, however, seems to explain the full range of a medium's abilities.

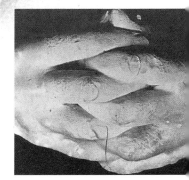

A Polish 'physical' medium called Franek Kluski was asked by investigators to *materialize* hands in a bowl of paraffin wax. Kluski did so, managing to keep the hands there until the wax had set. The investigators then used the imprint as a mould, and poured plaster into it to make a model of the hands.

An Indian medium called Sai Baba claims to be able to make objects materialize at will. Researchers have seen items ranging from a chunky necklace to oil appearing inexplicably from nowhere. Objects which appear at seances are called *apports.*

In 1898, a novel called 'The Wreck of the Titan' was published. The author, Morgan Robertson, claimed to have produced the book through automatic writing. It described how a luxury liner, called 'Titan', struck an iceberg and sank on its maiden voyage. In 1912, the luxury liner 'Titanic' had an identical accident on its maiden voyage and sank with terrible loss of life.

The Victorian novelist Charles Dickens died leaving his last book unfinished. Four years later, an American medium called T. P. James produced the last part of the book ('The Mystery of Edwin Drood'), claiming that it was dictated to him by Dickens's spirit. Although experts agreed that it could pass as Dickens's work, many were sceptical, saying that the new ending did not match Dickens's intentions for the story, which were known by his son and his illustrator.

AUTOMATIC WRITING

Many messages and even full-length books have been produced by people who claim that they were told what to write by spirits. This is called automatic writing – the writer has no control over what he or she is writing, but lets 'the spirits' take over their hand and guide it across the page. Sometimes, the messages are written in a language the writer does not understand, or even backwards. Often, the writer will be in a *trance* at the time, or under *hypnosis,* and will appear to take no notice whatever of what is being written.

One famous case of automatic writing happened in America at the beginning of the century. A medium called Pearl Curran began to receive messages through the *ouija board* (see page 26) from the spirit of a 17th-century British girl called Patience Worth. Patience said she had emigrated to America and had been killed by Indians there.

Over the next few years, Patience dictated several long historical novels. Although Mrs Curran did not have much education, the novels were of a high literary standard, and written in a style that only a language expert could have imitated, the English used being 17th century. Many people called the whole thing a fraud, but to this day, Patience Worth has baffled researchers, and convinced many that there is a life after death.

Cross-correspondences

Some of the strongest evidence for life after death was collected at the beginning of this century, when three separate *mediums* (one in America, one in England and one in India) all received messages from the same spirits through automatic writing The communicating spirits were all friends and had been famous psychical researchers when alive. The messages did not mean much on their own, but when put together they revealed references to books or other things which were known by the spirits when alive, but not by the mediums taking the messages.

The messages continued for several years, and they came to be known as the cross-correspondences. One of the dead researchers, Frederick Myers, mentioned how frustrating it was to communicate from the spirit world. He said it was like standing behind a sheet of frosted glass, trying to dictate to a secretary who was hard of hearing.

A 19th-century medium called Stainton Moses produced many examples of automatic writing. On one occasion, while he was holding the pen which was writing the messages, it suddenly jumped out of his hand and carried on writing by itself, clearly visible under a ray of light shining on it.

At the end of the last century, an 18-year old Canadian girl called Esther Cox was the victim of alarming poltergeist activities. One day, when the doctor came to visit, he was horrified to see, appearing on the wall before his eyes, the words, 'Esther Cox, you are mine to kill.' Direct writing such as this is often associated with poltergeist cases.

Direct writing

Direct writing is when writing appears without any visible being having written it. In some cases involving *poltergeists*, direct writing takes the form of graffiti, or short messages scrawled across the walls or on pieces of paper.

At the beginning of this century, some mediums used to hold drawing slates underneath the table during a *seance*. Although the medium's hands were still, the sound of scratching would be heard. When it stopped, the medium would produce the slate, which would have a message written on it. This practice soon went out of fashion, however, as it was difficult to prove that the mediums were not cheating in some way.

Automatic art and music

It is not only writing which is produced 'automatically', but also painting and music.

Rosemary Brown, from London, England, has produced many sheets of music which she claims have been dictated to her by dead masters such as Chopin, Liszt and Beethoven. They are dictated at great speed, and although Mrs Brown has no formal musical training herself, experts say that they are very good indeed. Mrs Brown is convinced that she is in communication with the dead – she even mentioned at one point that Beethoven's English was improving!

From the subconscious?

A number of experts, along with some of those who produce automatic writing, believe that it really comes from the writers' minds, and not from spirits. It is thought that, in a certain state, the mind is capable of imitating the works of great masters, and that we all possess a great deal more knowledge than we think we do, which can surface from the *subconscious* in the form of automatic writing, painting or music.

Some other cases of automatic writing seem to be the result of *telepathy*. In 1922, for instance, a group of six *spiritualists* met at a house in Flushing, Holland. Using a device similar to a *ouija board,* they picked up a short poem in English. Later, it was discovered that a boy who lived opposite had been reading the same poem at the time of the meeting.

A Brazilian man called Luiz Gasparetto has painted many pictures which he claims are the works of famous dead painters. In 1978, he demonstrated his gift on TV, producing 21 pictures in 75 minutes. Sometimes he also paints two pictures at once – one with his left hand and the other with his right!

DOWSING

Dowsing or 'divining' is the ability to find water, metal, or just about anything hidden under the ground. Often, this is done by walking over the area, holding a forked twig made of springy wood such as hazel. When the substance being looked for is underfoot, the twig will bend down or up, or twist in the dowser's hands.

Some dowsers use metal rods, or pendulums – which are small round weights such as a button, on the end of a piece of thread. Those who use pendulums often do not need to go to the area at all, but they dowse over a map of the area with just as much success.

In America, Canada and Russia, many companies employ dowsers as a matter of course if, for instance, they are looking for water supplies for new factories. Dowsers not only find underground streams, but many can also pinpoint exactly how far down they are, in what direction the water is flowing, and how pure it is.

Other things that dowsers have found are gold and other precious metals, ancient archaeological sites, lost objects and people, and some have discovered huge oil fields, especially in America. One man, Clayton McDowell, saved a school in Illinois from financial ruin by locating oil below its grounds. The oil well set up on the site produces $500-worth of oil every day.

Theories about dowsing

A small number of researchers think that dowsers use *psychic* ability to 'see' what lies in the ground. This view is supported by the fact that many dowsers work from maps alone.

It is now generally believed that dowsing is basically the ability of the human body to respond to tiny electrical impulses emitted by the water or object being dowsed. For example, if a dowser walks over water, they are unconsciously aware of the electrical field surrounding it and their muscles twitch very slightly. This small movement causes the hazel twig or pendulum to move much more noticeably. But this does not explain the success of those who dowse over maps or the fact that children are better than adults at dowsing.

Hand tremblers

Some dowsers use only their hands when they are dowsing. This takes a lot of practice, as it is much

Ancient Greek priests used to dowse for information by putting an image of a god on their shoulders and waiting for it to answer their questions. If the god pulled them forward it meant yes; if it pulled them back it meant no.

This 16th-century drawing shows people dowsing for metal in Germany. The two dowsers shown are using forked hazel twigs. Nowadays, dowsing for metal and oil is usually done over a map.

In 1952, a British army colonel called Harry Grattan dowsed for a water-supply for a new headquarters at Reindalin in West Germany. He found a huge supply of fresh, soft water covering an area of 75 square

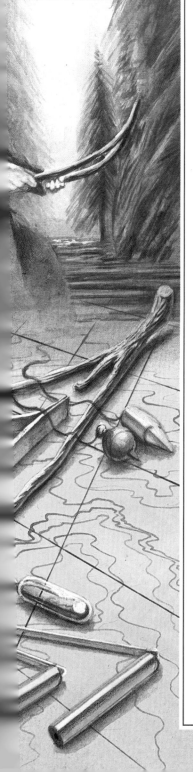

kilometres, close to the hard water supply used by the nearby town. Because he covered a large area, Harry Grattan dowsed on horseback, holding his hazel stick straight out in front of him.

more difficult to detect a definite movement of the hands than it is to watch a twig or pendulum. In some tribal communities, local dowsers (or 'diviners'), who use their skill to find criminals or lost objects, identify the cause of disease and predict the future, are called hand-tremblers, because they use only the movement of their hands, rather than any equipment. The diviners of the Navaho American Indians put pollen on their hands and go into a *trance* before they dowse.

Medical dowsing

In the 1920s, a dowser called the Abbé Mermet developed the idea of dowsing for illnesses and their cures, called *radiesthesia*. Although it is dismissed by many doctors, there are some who use it very successfully. A doctor called Abrams even found a way of diagnosing illnesses without the patient being there – all that was needed was a drop of their blood, or a lock of hair. A pendulum held over it would then 'answer' questions about the disease and its cure.

Tom Lethbridge

One of the most important psychical researchers this century was Tom Lethbridge who lived in Cornwall, England. Apart from developing theories about the nature of ghosts – he thought they may be recordings which can be 'played back' in the right conditions – he also had many ideas about dowsing.

Most of Lethbridge's ideas were based on his own experiences, of which one of the most alarming happened at the Merry Maidens stone circle in Cornwall. He was holding his pendulum over one of the stones, and touching the stone with his other hand. As the pendulum rotated, he suddenly felt a sensation like an electric shock going through his whole body. This became stronger, but he managed to carry on dowsing. Because of this, he came to believe in the force which seems to come from ancient standing stones at certain times. He also believed that dowsing was the body's reaction to forces from the earth.

Lethbridge also studied the use of the pendulum. He found that, by altering the length of the string according to what he was dowsing, the pendulum could be used to find literally anything, once you knew the length, or 'rate', for it. Even emotions such as happiness and anger responded to a certain pendulum length.

A French dowser called Joseph Treyve used to swing his pendulum over a map of the local woods to find wild boars for hunting. He was manager of a horticultural centre, and one day, when one of his workmen failed to turn up, he found him in a local cafe by holding his pendulum over a street-plan of the town.

Sometimes, the 'force' of ancient monuments such as standing stones is so great that a dowser can be knocked to the ground when approaching them. A pendulum can be used to determine the age of the stones.

In 1983, Carol Compton, a nanny in Italy, was brought to court accused of deliberately starting fires in the homes where she worked. During the trial, however, it emerged that the fires behaved oddly – one did not burn the spot where it started, for instance, although surrounding furniture was charred. It was believed by many that Carol had unconscious PK ability to start fires.

In the 1920s, a Brazilian psychic, Carlos Mirabelli, performed many amazing PK feats under test conditions. He could levitate, and produce fully-formed 'materializations' of people who had recently died. He was also said to be able to play billiards without touching any ball with his cue, and once, at a banquet, an invisible hand played a march on a row of bottles and glasses. In later tests, he moved many objects from a distance, even uprooting flowers in a window-box before an astonished researcher.

MIND OVER MATTER

'Mind over matter' is the ability to make objects move without touching them. This is done by concentrating hard and willing them to move. Researchers call it PK, which stands for *psychokinesis*. Because it is related to many aspects of ESP (*extrasensory perception* – see page 34), PK and ESP are sometimes called by the joint name of *psi* (pronounced 'sigh').

PK can take many forms. Some *mediums* display it during *seances,* claiming that it is the spirits working through them. On those occasions, tables can move on their own, or musical instruments play by themselves, and sometimes objects may fly around the room. PK is also thought to be the source of *poltergeist* activities (see pages 10–11)

Uri Geller

The most famous modern *psychic* is the Israeli Uri Geller, who has appeared on TV world-wide to display his powers of PK and ESP. Although there are many who say that he is a cheat, thousands have testified that cutlery and keys bent, and broken clocks and watches mysteriously began to work, during Geller's appearances on TV or the radio. One person even claimed that their car engine started of its own accord during a Geller interview on British TV.

Most of Geller's successes are with metal, and he claims that his power is strongest when he is near metal, or touching it. Once, while bending a key by stroking it lightly, he placed his foot on a nearby metal radiator to increase his powers.

Geller first became famous in the early 1970s, and since then he has been subjected to many tests by researchers, most of whom were satisfied that he does have psychic powers. One of Geller's main enemies was the American magician 'The Amazing Randi' who went to great lengths to show that Geller's feats were tricks that could be reproduced by a good magician.

Although Geller's reputation has now been damaged, there are still many who are convinced of his powers. After his appearances on TV, many children claimed to be able to bend metal in the same way. The children were tested, and researchers were led to believe that Geller's PK powers were not unique, and that many people possessed them to a certain degree.

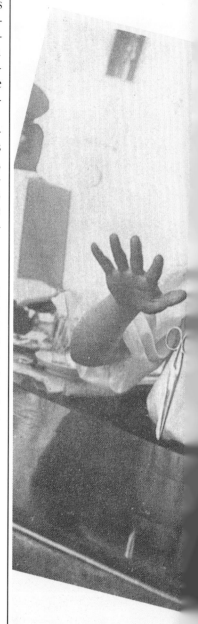

A Polish medium called Stanislawa Tomczyk could levitate small objects between her hands, such as small balls and cigarettes. It looked as if she was controlling them by threads.

Who has PK ability?

There is no special type of person who has PK ability, although some tests have shown that those who believe in the power are more likely to display it in test conditions. Another important factor is that the start of PK powers often coincides with some great shock in a person's life, as if that 'opens up' their psychic powers.

One woman who tried to develop PK powers failed until the day she received a phone call to say that a relative was dead. After that, when she tried to pick up a plastic bottle it jumped away from her as if it had a life of its own.

Sometimes shocks have the reverse effect. An American student, Hubert Pearce, whose psychic powers seemed to be very developed, found that they deserted him after he had some bad news from home.

The 'electric children'

There have been cases of children who have displayed an alarming kind of PK. Whenever they went near furniture, it would jump away from them. It was as if the children were permanently charged with some sort of static electricity that affected anything they went near. In the 1840s, a 14-year-old French girl, Angélique Cottin, found that whenever she went to sit down, the chair or sofa would move away with such force that no one could hold it. When she was taken to Paris for investigations, however, the mysterious force stopped as suddenly as it had begun, before tests could be successfully completed. Like many poltergeist cases, it lasted only a few months, and although Angélique was the focus of the force, she had no control over it at all.

Levitation

Levitation is the ability to defy gravity and make objects, or yourself, rise up from the ground. In the past, many holy people had this ability. For instance, Joseph of Copertino, who lived in 17th-century Italy, frequently levitated while at church. Floating over the heads of all the congregation, he would end up hovering above the altar, sometimes staying there for 15 minutes at a time. On one occasion, he floated up into the branches of an olive tree and could not get down again! Since then, many mediums have displayed amazing levitating powers.

A 16th-century nun called Teresa of Avila was so embarrassed by her spontaneous levitation that she held herself down while at prayer to avoid floating upwards out of control.

During one of Daniel Dunglas Home's *seances* (see page 26), a woman was reportedly levitated in her chair a few centimetres from the ground. It happened again, and this time the lady knelt in the chair so that the others could see all its legs and confirm that neither she nor anyone else was cheating.

as if they were puppets. On one occasion a teaspoon threw itself out of a glass after she had concentrated on it. She always performed while in a *trance*.

In 1912, in Munich, Germany, some amazing ESP tests were made on a group of horses, known as the 'Elberfield horses'. Several of them could solve mathematical problems in seconds, rapping out the answers with their hooves. One investigator laid out three number cards face-down in front of one of the horses, Muhamed. He had not looked at the cards first, but to the investigator's astonishment, Muhamed rapped out the numbers written on the cards correctly.

In the 19th century, an Italian woman discovered that she could read with her ears! During a test, lines of print were held to the side of her head, and she read them as if she was using her eyes. It has often been found that people (often those who are blind) have the ability to read and 'see' colours by touching them with their finger tips. This kind of clairvoyance is called 'finger-tip vision'.

ESP

ESP (*extra-sensory perception*) is the ability to acquire information without using the ordinary five senses – sight, hearing, taste, touch and smell.

There are three main types of ESP. The first is *clairvoyance,* where people become aware of events or objects without seeing them with their eyes, although they may 'see' them in their minds. The second type of ESP is *telepathy,* where thoughts and ideas are transferred between minds without being spoken or written, and sometimes over great distances. *Precognition* – the ability to see events before they happen – is the third type of ESP. You can find out about this on pages 38–39.

Clairvoyance

Clairvoyance is a fairly common ability – many people have experienced it at least once in their lives. Some *psychics* can even control it and use it at will. Recently, for instance, a Dutchman called Gerard Croiset used his gift to help police find missing people. Sometimes, if a person was dead, he would be able to 'see' where the body was and tell the police where to look. In some cases of kidnapping, he could also see the whole route taken by the kidnappers. Croiset said that his information came to him like film-clips inside his head.

Another psychic ability related to clairvoyance is 'hearing voices'. This is called *clairaudience,* and *mediums* are the most likely people to experience it. Other people, however, not usually psychic, claim to have an 'inner voice' that gives them information such as a warning of danger. The former British Prime Minister Winston Churchill claimed often to hear such a voice. On one occasion, during the Second World War, it told him to climb into a different seat of his car from his usual one. A bomb exploded near the car on the journey, lifting it onto two wheels. Churchill believed that if he had been sitting in his normal seat, the car would have overturned. As it was, his weight kept it upright.

Another fairly common psychic experience is to smell or taste something that is not there. Often those who think they have been in contact with a ghost do not actually claim to have seen it. Instead, they claim to have smelt a strong scent of, for example, violets, or felt a light touch on their arm. This is called *clairsentience.*

Emmanuel Swedenborg, the 18th-century philosopher, had many psychic experiences. One of the most vivid occurred when he was staying in Gothenburg in Sweden. He described a fire

which was raging at that very minute through Stockholm, 480 kilometres away. His description was later confirmed in every detail by a courier from Stockholm.

Remote viewing

Remote viewing is the ability to 'see' places without actually being there at the time. It is as if the mind travels there without the body. A man named Ingo Swann, for instance, was able to describe faraway places in accurate detail without having been to them. He even claimed to have 'travelled' to Mars and Venus. Some of his information about these places was proved to be inaccurate, however, after space probes landed on both planets.

Telepathy

Telepathy is difficult to control as it needs the participation of two or more people – one actively trying to transmit their thoughts, and the other trying to receive and understand them. Spontaneous telepathy, however, is one of the most common psychic experiences there is and often happens between close friends or relatives. Mothers often seem to have telepathic communication with their children, for instance.

Some people also claim telepathy with their animals. The author Rider Haggard dreamed one night that his daughter's dog was lying by a river, dying. Later, the dog was found dead in the river – it was believed that he had been knocked by a train to the river's edge before being swept away and drowned. Rider Haggard thought that the dog was trying to communicate his predicament to him.

Testing for ESP

A standard laboratory test for ESP is to use cards, called *zener cards,* which each have a different symbol – a square, a cross, a circle, a star or wavy lines. The 'subject' (the person being tested) has to guess which symbol is on the card the investigator picks up.

Nowadays, ESP testing is often done using specially developed machines. One machine randomly selects a zener symbol, and the subject presses a button on a second machine, to guess which symbol has come up.

This kind of testing has also been used for telepathy. In one test, the investigator pictured the zener symbols one by one, and the subject had to read his thoughts.

Although test conditions for ESP are usually strict, many scientists are unwilling to accept that ESP exists. It is, however, one of the more accepted areas of the supernatural.

In some tribal communities, *shamans* (see page 22) practise clairvoyance as part of their day-to-day lives. African *witch doctors* do the same. At the beginning of this century, a French missionary described how he had tested a witch doctor's power by asking him to contact a man who lived 150 kilometres away and tell him to bring gun cartridges to a meeting that had been organized three days later. The man arrived with the cartridges, saying that he had heard the witch doctor's voice telling him to bring them.

TRAVELLING THROUGH SPACE AND TIME

Some people claim to have defied all normal laws of space and time and travelled many miles in just a few seconds – as if by *magic*. This is called *teleportation,* or translocation. Although a person who is teleported is not usually aware of controlling or willing the experience in any way, it often happens to those who are known to be *psychic*. Because of this, researchers think that teleportation must be linked with psychic ability and controlled, unconsciously, by the mind.

The Israeli psychic Uri Geller (see page 32) has experienced a number of teleportations. In 1973, for instance, he was walking along a New York street when he felt a strange pull upwards on his body. Seconds later, he found himself crashing through the porch screen in a friend's house 60 kilometres away.

In the past, it was thought that fairies were responsible for spiriting people away whenever they felt like it. One 17th-century story, for instance, tells of an Englishman, Lord Duffus, who was walking in some fields near his house. Suddenly, he found himself in Paris, in the King of France's cellar, holding a silver cup. Afterwards he said that when he was whisked away, he heard voices saying 'Horse and Hattock', which was popularly believed to be the fairy code for teleportation.

Teleportation of objects

When objects appear from nowhere, or seem to travel impossibly between rooms in a building, they are called *apports*. Some *mediums* produce apports during *seances*, although they do not always intend to – it often seems to be a by-product of psychic ability.

An English medium called Stainton Moses, who conducted seances in the 1870s, was apparently plagued by apports that he could not control. On one occasion, a large candlestick, which normally stood in the next room, appeared and hit Moses very hard on the head.

Recently, the Indian medium Sai Baba (see page 27) seems to be one of the few people who can produce apports at will.

On the 25th October 1593, a soldier who had been on duty in the Philippines suddenly appeared 15,000 kilometres away in Mexico City. When questioned, he seemed confused, saying that moments before he had been on duty as usual when the Governor of the Philippines was suddenly assassinated. Later reports proved his story to be true.

In 1871, it was claimed that Mrs Guppy, a 20-stone (127 kg) English medium, was teleported, in her underclothes, from her London home right into the middle of a seance in another London house. The report of this first 'human apport' became a popular joke for a time, and was generally disbelieved, despite there being several witnesses to the event.

On Iona, an island off the West of Scotland, a scene from the 10th century has been re-enacted several times. On one occasion, a man who was living at Iona Abbey set off for a walk. After a while, he noticed that the landscape looked different and that some cottages were missing. Then, arriving at the North beach, he suddenly saw a fleet of 14 Viking longboats. They landed, and he watched as a group of monks on the shore were slaughtered by Vikings, who then raced off towards the Abbey. Later, they reappeared with Abbey treasures and sailed away, leaving the Abbey ablaze. The scene then returned to normal, and the astonished man later found out that such an invasion had really happened.

Researchers baffled

Some researchers believe that teleportation is impossible, and that those who claim to have experienced it are either frauds or mistaken. Even those who are willing to believe in it find it difficult to explain. Some think that in order to teleport, a person would have to 'dematerialize', or go through a time barrier or into another dimension, simply through mind power. It certainly sounds unconvincing, but there are too many accounts for the whole idea to be dismissed completely.

Time travel

Normally, we think of time as a series of building blocks – one thing happens after another, and there is no going back. However, some scientists say that this view is wrong, and some people have had experiences which certainly suggest that it is.

In 1901, two English university teachers, Charlotte Moberly and Eleanor Jourdain, visited the palace at Versailles in France, where Louis XVI and Marie Antoinette lived just before the French Revolution in 1789.

As the ladies walked about the garden, they felt oddly depressed and 'dream-like'. Then they heard music and saw a number of people in 18th-century dress. Two strangely-clothed gardeners gave them directions, and Miss Moberly saw a woman sitting drawing close by. There was also a wedding party which they followed for a while.

There had been no rehearsals for plays or pageants that day, and the ladies could only conclude later that they really had had a glimpse of the past. When they returned home, they wrote a book about their experience, called 'An Adventure'. Many people were reluctant to believe the story, and various explanations were offered. Now, however, fresh evidence has come to light. It seems that the two ladies accurately describe things that, at the time of their experience, nobody knew about 18th-century France.

Recordings?

Scenes such as the one above are usually linked to one particular place, and, when people witness them, it is as if they have stumbled into the past by accident. There seems to be no rational explanation for this defiance of time, unless the scenes are somehow recordings (see pages 4–5) which are on such a large scale that they can affect several kilometres of landscape.

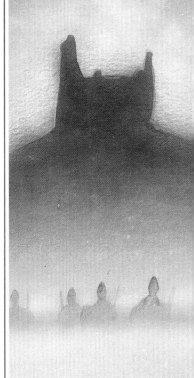

A few days after the First World War ended in 1918, two soldiers went looking for cooking equipment at an inn near the French/Belgian border. Suddenly, 20 German cavalry rode silently out of the nearby wood. They were met by a company of French soldiers, but just before their weapons clashed, both companies completely vanished and the scene returned to normal. The two men later discovered that dead French and German soldiers were buried close by.

Oracles in Ancient Greece were consulted by many for advice, or knowledge about the future. The oracles themselves were gods and they usually spoke through a woman who acted as a priest at the oracle's shrine. One oracle at Dodona, however, was an oak tree. It answered questions by rustling its leaves, or sometimes through the doves that sat on its branches. Priests were trained to interpret these answers.

At the beginning of this century, an English Bishop's wife, Mrs Atlay, dreamed that she found a pig in her dining room, standing between the table and the sideboard. The next morning, after prayers, she went into the dining room, and was astonished to find that there really was a pig standing there. Apparently it had earlier escaped from its sty.

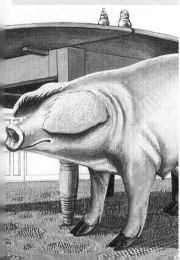

SEEING THE FUTURE

Many people have had *premonitions* about the future – which means 'seeing' events before they happen. Researchers call this *precognition* ('knowing beforehand'), and those who experience it are said to have 'second sight', which means that they see things not with their eyes, but with their minds.

Premonitions come in all forms – they can be dreams, visions, or just vague feelings that something will happen. They can also predict a large range of events, from an air disaster to something quite ordinary, such as 'knowing' that a letter from a friend will arrive the next day.

In some countries, second sight has always been regarded as a natural part of life. For example, in regions as far apart as Siberia and South America, tribal priests/magicians called *shamans* (see page 22) still use their *psychic* powers to solve all sorts of problems that people bring them.

Prophets

In the past, those who saw the future regularly and on a grand scale were called *prophets*. Many of them were religious leaders, such as Moses in the Old Testament of the Bible, and Muhammed, who founded Islam. It was thought that God spoke through prophets to tell people how he wanted them to live and warn them of what would happen if they disobeyed.

Not all prophets, however, were religious. A Frenchman called Michel de Nostradame (known as Nostradamus) published almost 1,000 prophecies between 1555 and 1566. They were all written in four-line verses, and although they often did not give exact dates of events, many seem to have been fulfilled. Some of the events which he seemed to prophesy were the Great Fire of London in 1666, the French Revolution in 1789 and the advance of Hitler into Poland in 1939, which started the Second World War.

The Fatima prophecies

In 1917, in Fatima, Portugal, three children claimed to have seen a vision of Virgin Mary,

Sometimes, accidents are avoided through premonitions. One man, while on holiday in Scotland, sent his daughter out for a walk. Suddenly, he 'knew' that she was in danger, and sent a servant who found her going to the beach to sit on some stones by a railway bridge. Later, they heard that an engine fell off the bridge and onto the stones at the time she would have been there.

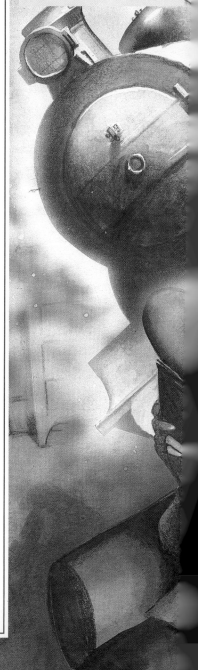

who told them three 'secrets' about the future. The first was apparently a vision of hell. The second predicted the start of the Second World War, which began 22 years later. The third secret was sent to the Pope in a sealed envelope, and was kept unopened in the Vatican until 1960, when Pope John XXIII read it. Witnesses said that the contents made the Pope nearly faint with terror. The third secret has never been made public, but it is thought to be a prediction of some terrible event that is yet to happen.

Premonitions in dreams

Most premonitions come in the form of dreams which are sometimes repeated night after night until the event happens. In 1979, for instance, an office worker from Ohio, USA, had the same nightmare for ten nights in a row about a DC-10 aeroplane which crashed upside-down and in flames on an airport runway. A few days later, an identical accident took place at Chicago's O'Hare airport, killing 275 people.

Investigating precognition

Laboratory experiments have been carried out to see if people can really predict the future. In one experiment, a panel of coloured lights were set to go on and off in a random way. Students had to guess which light would come on next. Some often guessed correctly.

In another experiment, the Dutch psychic Gerard Croiset (see page 34) had to describe the next person to sit in a chair which had been preselected by the researcher. He gave many accurate descriptions with details such as height, hair colour, clothes, and even events from the person's life.

Unconscious premonitions

It seems that many people, without being aware of it, can sense approaching danger. A study made in the 1950s, for instance, showed that the number of people travelling on trains that crash is often much less than the usual number of people on the same train. In 1952, for instance, nine people were on a train that crashed. For the fortnight before the crash, however, it was found that, on average, 55 people normally did that journey every day.

In 1934, a British pilot, Victor Goddard, was lost over Scotland in his biplane, after spending the afternoon at the abandoned Drem airport. Suddenly, he caught sight of the airport and was astonished to see it transformed. Light streamed from it, and mechanics were busy working on planes. Four years later, Drem was just as Goddard had seen it that night – it seemed that he had taken a flight into the future.

In 1896, a German woman called Madame de Ferriem had a nightmarish vision of a coal-mining disaster in which many people were killed. She pinpointed the area as Dux (now Duchkov) in Czechoslovakia, and the season of the year it happened. She also saw details of the people's clothing. Four years later, the disaster happened as she had 'seen' it.

Mademoiselle Lenormand, born in 1772, was acclaimed as France's queen of fortune-tellers. Using several methods, she predicted the marriage of Napoleon Bonaparte and Josephine, and advised them several times throughout their lives. After the French Revolution, she was put in prison for predicting the death of Robespierre – one of the Revolution's leaders. While in prison, she saved a woman from execution. In a note, she told her to pretend to be ill when they came to take her to another prison. If she did this, she would live long – if not, she would be guillotined.

An astrologer called Jean Stoeffler worked out that he was fated to die from a blow on the head on a certain day in 1530. When the day arrived, he stayed indoors to try to cheat the prediction. As he reached up for a book on a shelf, however, the bookcase toppled and fell on his head, killing him instantly!

FORTUNE-TELLING

People have always been curious about the future, and have wanted to know what will happen to them. Because of this, many systems to help us see the future have been developed and used, sometimes for thousands of years. Some of these systems are relatively simple, such as reading patterns of tea leaves in the bottom of a cup, or interpreting playing cards symbolically. *Tarot cards,* which were developed especially for fortune-telling, contain different symbols representing possible future destinies, such as great wealth. They are dealt by the fortune-teller, who then reads and interprets the client's cards.

Astrology and the I Ching

Astrology is based on the ancient belief that people are affected by the movement of the planets. Their position at the time of a person's birth is thought by astrologers to have great influence over their future.

Astrologers draw up charts for people, called *horoscopes,* which often seem to give an accurate description of them and sometimes predict their future. A shorthand version of astrology is the horoscopes in the daily papers, shown under the 12 signs of the zodiac – the groups of stars that are said to have particular influence over us. Everyone is born in one of these signs, which has general characteristics associated with it. Gemini (the twins), for instance, is supposed to denote a person who is intelligent, but never finishes things.

Many people have dismissed astrology, yet recent studies have shown that some people are affected by the full moon – it makes some aggressive, for instance. Often people born under the influence of Saturn tend to be quiet, while those born under Mars are outgoing.

The *I Ching,* like astrology, is an ancient system, used for fortune-telling and as a source of advice. It is used mainly in China, and consists of a series of patterns called hexagrams, each made up of six lines. After asking the I Ching any personal question concerning the future, or a decision you are trying to make, you find the right hexagram by tossing coins or twigs. The hexagram's meaning should contain advice about the question you asked.

The Romans were very *superstitious.* Many emperors had personal astrologers who advised them when making decisions. There were also priests and priestesses who interpreted *omens* from the gods. A haruspex, for instance, examined the liver of a sacrificed animal for favourable signs. Augurs interpreted flights of birds, and thunder. Sybils lived in caves and wrote predictions, usually concerning the fate of politicians and emperors.

Palmistry

Palmistry is based on the belief that the lines on the palms of your hands represent your whole life – past, present and future. Your left hand is supposed to be the destiny you were born with, and your right hand is said to represent how your character and destiny might change or have changed due to circumstance and decisions you make in your life. Palm-reading is thousands of years old and it is still popular today all over the world.

One of the most successful palm-readers this century was a man called Cheiro, who read the palms of the rich and famous. He is said to have foretold in detail the murder of the Russian 'mad monk' Rasputin. He also predicted the Russian Revolution of 1917, and the Czar's death.

Numerology

Numerologists say that every number has a special meaning, and the character and future of a person can be worked out from the numerical value of their name and the numbers in their date of birth.

Numerology also draws links between the lives of people. For instance, two American presidents, Lincoln and Kennedy, both had seven letters in their surnames and were assassinated on the fifth day of the week. Their murderers both had 15 letters in their names, and one was born in 1839, and the other in 1939. The vice presidents at the time, Andrew Johnson and Lyndon Johnson, were born in 1808 and 1908 respectively. Although many would call it coincidence, numerologists would argue that the similarity of numbers between the two ill-fated presidents was no accident.

Bone-casting

The *witch doctors* (or 'nganga') of African tribes use a system of *bone-casting* to answer problems brought to them. The bones, called hakata, are either real or carved from ivory or hard wood. There are four bones in a set and each has a special design. When the bones are thrown to the ground, they can fall into 16 possible patterns, which the witch doctor interprets, often while in a *trance.* The way the bones fall is thought to be controlled by spirits.

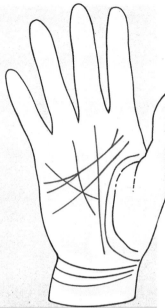

Palm-reading is now thought by some doctors to help with diagnosing illness. All the tiny lines and crosses on your palm are claimed to be an indication of what sort of illnesses you will tend to get and at what age. Although this idea is not yet generally accepted, more research is being carried out.

Queen Elizabeth I of England had a personal astrologer called Dr John Dee. He set favourable days for Elizabethan ships to set sail, advised the Queen on how to conduct the war against Spain, and accurately predicted the execution of Mary Queen of Scots.

Under hypnosis, an English woman, Naomi Henry, became Mary Cohen who had lived in Cork, Ireland, in the 18th century. Answering the hypnotist's questions, 'Mary' described her life until the point when she was 70 years old 'and very ill'. When the hypnotist asked more questions, there was no reply, and Naomi herself stopped breathing. It seemed she had reached the point where 'Mary' had died. The hypnotist managed to call her back, but it was a severe shock to all present.

A four-year-old Indian boy, Bishen Chand, claimed that he was the dead nephew of a man who had lived in a town 30 miles from his own. Bishen was eventually taken to the town, where the detailed descriptions he had given of the people and places proved to be accurate. At the house where he said he had lived, he met a relative of his former 'uncle'. The relative showed him a faded photograph and Bishen pointed out his former self without hesitation in front of a curious crowd.

PAST LIVES

Some people believe that they have lived before – that their soul, in other bodies, has had many past lives, stretching over thousands of years. This is called *reincarnation* and it is a basic belief in religions such as Buddhism and Hinduism. (see page 14).

In normal waking life, most people cannot remember anything about their past lives, but, under *hypnosis,* some can be taken back slowly until they seem to become totally different people and relive some of their former experiences.

What convinces many researchers that past lives are genuine is that people often give many accurate historical details about their past life, sometimes in another country and usually in a different century. Sometimes they speak in a language they do not normally know, or show knowledge about things that they have never learnt. Some people are taken back through several past lives. One woman has 'remembered' 11 lives – nine of them lived as a man.

Jane Evans

Sometimes, those who remember past lives give historical details which are not in any history book because they are not yet discovered. A woman called Jane Evans, for instance, described how she had been a Jewess, 'Rebecca', living in 12th-century York. She had a vivid memory of being chased with her family by a group of anti-Jewish Christians. They hid in a crypt under a nearby church until the danger was passed. Puzzled researchers could find no record of the crypt. Shortly afterwards, however, it was discovered for the first time since the 12th century, indicating that 'Rebecca' knew more about the time than Jane Evans, or the historians, could have known.

Walking into the past

Some people do not need to be hypnotised to remember a former life. Without warning, they have 'walked into the past', not as an observer, but as a character of that time. An Englishman, Major McDonough, had such an experience while in India. He was standing on a ridge, looking down into a valley, when he suddenly saw many ancient Greek soldiers who were camping there. The next thing he knew, he was

An English soldier called Alex Ainscough had a strange experience in Rouen, France, in 1918, at the end of the First World War. As he walked through the town, he had an odd feeling that it was familiar, although he had never been there before. Suddenly, he found himself marching at the head of a column of soldiers. He was tall and dressed in chainmail. Somehow he knew that he was going to see the burning of Joan of Arc. When he got to the end of the street, there was a market, and on a tablet above a piece of pavement it was written that Joan of Arc died there — a fact that Alex Ainscough did not know.

amongst them, and a soldier himself. Walking over to a group, he saw that they were standing by a rock on which was written an inscription to mark the death of one of Alexander the Great's generals. The inscription was freshly made and the soldiers all seemed sad. To the Major's surprise, he found he could read the Greek words easily, although he had never studied the language. A moment later, the scene returned to normal and he was back on top of the ridge.

The Major later explored the valley, and found the rock almost overgrown by the jungle. The inscription was worn, but he could read enough to know that it was the same one he had seen before, which, he reckoned, had been originally written in 329 BC.

Unconscious memories

Although the evidence for past lives seems strong, there are some experts who believe that all such experiences come from the memory, which, in certain conditions, can recall an amazing amount of information which people do not even know they have. This is called *cryptomnesia*. (Some even think that memories, like eye and hair colour, can be passed on to children before they are born.)

Under hypnosis, some people have 'remembered' experiences which have turned out to be from something they have read, seen or heard years before but have forgotten. In one case, a servant girl, who could neither read nor write, spoke in fluent Greek and Hebrew while she was delirious with fever. It was later discovered that she had worked for a vicar who used to read aloud to himself in those languages. The girl had unconsciously remembered it all.

Police departments in New York and Israel now have permanent staff trained to hypnotise witnesses who cannot remember details about suspected criminals. In 1982, for instance, two women saw a man being shot dead in New York. Questioned by specially trained police hypnotists, one of the women gave a minute description of the killer while in a hypnotic trance. She even remembered what kind of spectacle frames he had. And in Israel, a bus-driver whose bus was bombed by terrorists could remember under hypnosis everything about every person who had got on and off the bus before the bomb went off. His description of one man led the police to the bomber.

A 13-year-old Finnish girl claimed, under hypnosis, to be 'Dorothy', the daughter of an English inn-keeper, born in 1139. Although the girl knew almost no English, she sang a rare 12th-century English song, called 'The Cuckoo Song'. A few years later, hypnotised again, the girl revealed that she had seen the song by chance in a library book called 'The story of Music'. Somehow, she had amazingly remembered the whole song after only a glance, even though it was in a language she did not know.

The researchers working on the Raudive tapes have been helped by Rufus the dog. He can hear some voices which are out of the researchers' range, and barks to draw their attention to them.

This infra-red photograph taken in 1953 at a *seance* in Pennsylvania, USA, is claimed to be of a spirit guide called Silver Belle. She *materialized* from a cloud of ectoplasm while the *medium* sat in a cubicle. (Infra-red films are used because they detect heat, not light, and can be used in dark rooms.)

CAPTURING GHOSTS

Since the end of the last century, many people have tried to prove that ghosts exist by capturing them on photograph or tape. There have been so many fakes, however, that even the few which do seem genuine are regarded with suspicion by experts.

For some reason, ghosts seem unwilling to be caught on any kind of electronic equipment – there have been many cases where cameras and tapes set up in haunted houses have mysteriously gone wrong at the crucial moment.

The Raudive tapes

Recently, the most successful evidence that ghosts could be taped was collected by a Latvian psychologist, Konstantin Raudive. Over a number of years, until his death in 1974, he collected over 100,000 messages on tape which, he claimed, came from the spirit world. On one 18-minute recording, 200 separate voices were counted, 27 of which were clearly audible to anyone with normal hearing. Raudive's spirits always spoke in a variety of languages – sometimes several in the course of a single sentence. Often, the messages were difficult to interpret, but the spirits were always anxious to emphasize that there really was a spirit world. Sometimes well-known voices would be heard – Stalin apparently complained of the heat in the spirit world!

One English researcher called David Ellis believes that the voices are simply caused by interference from nearby radio stations. Raudive, however, recorded the voices in several different ways to avoid this charge, and was examined and tested by many researchers who became convinced that the voices could not come from a normal source.

Photographs

Most 'ghost photographs' which have not been proved to be fakes were taken when the photographer was unaware until the film was developed that there was anything strange there at all. In 1891, for instance, a woman called Sybell Corbet took a photograph of the library of Combermere Abbey, England –

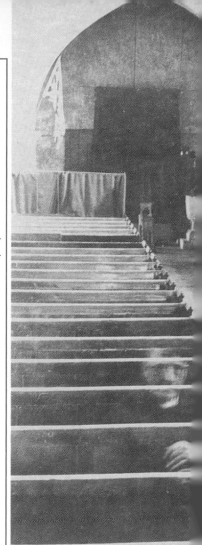

This picture was taken in England in 1956. It shows the inside of Eastry church – with the addition of a ghostly figure seated in a pew close to the photographer. The photographer was alone in the church at the time.

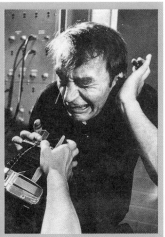

Ted Serios, the American 'thoughtographer', demonstrating his technique of grimacing in front of the camera while taking a thoughtograph.

home of Lord Combermere, who had died a few days previously. When the photograph was developed, it plainly showed the shadowy figure of a legless man, sitting in Lord Combermere's favourite chair. Although many were convinced that this was Lord Combermere's ghost, there were also many who pointed out that as the photograph was exposed for an hour – during which time Miss Corbett left the room – there was plenty of time for someone to come in, sit down for a few seconds, then leave. The result would have been a shadowy outline like the one on the photograph.

The difficulty of photographing ghosts has always been that it is easy to tamper with cameras and film and produce very convincing fakes. Some people have taken fraud even further. In the 1920s, a cleaning lady called Ada Emma Deane produced many photographs which, she claimed, were of dead soldiers, taken at the London war memorial. Many of the families of the soldiers believed that she had really produced pictures of their dead loved ones. Eventually, however, a press agency announced that Mrs Deane had used photographs of living sportsmen which they had on their files. She cut out the faces, stuck cotton wool around them, and photographed them, producing the effect of faces staring out of heavenly clouds.

Thoughtography

Some researchers believe that it is possible to 'think' an image onto a piece of film, so that a photograph is produced of something which is not there. Ted Serios, an American, produced many of these – called *'thoughtographs'* – in the 1960s. He would stare at the camera, then, with an enormous burst of energy, would try to project pictures onto the film. Serios often used a cardboard tube while producing his thoughtographs, which he would hold in front of the camera and stare down. Some accused him of hiding tiny slides in the tube which were then photographed by the camera. His researcher, however, stated that he often produced images when not using this device, and anyway, it was always checked before and after each session.

Some researchers believe that seemingly genuine photographs of 'ghosts' may in fact be thoughtographs – projected unconsciously by someone with psychic powers.

Some of the fake spirit photographs taken by Ada Emma Deane. They actually show the faces of living sportsmen, taken from the files of a press agency.

GLOSSARY

Alchemy The half-scientific, half-magical study of how to change metals into gold.

Angels Good spirits which protect against evil and provide help.

Animism The belief that everything and everyone has a living spirit, or soul.

Apparition Appearance of a ghost or supernatural being.

Apport An object that appears as if from nowhere, or moves from place to place without being touched.

Astrology The study of how the planets influence the character and future of people.

Autoscopy The ability to diagnose illness through psychic means.

Banshee A fairy woman, seen or heard by Irish families at the time of a death.

Black magic Magic used for evil purposes, eg to injure people or to gain power.

Bone-casting A method of divination, to find, for instance, the cause of an illness, used by tribal witch doctors (Nganga).

Bone-pointing The act of pointing a bone at a person for the purpose of killing them, used by Australian Aborigines either maliciously or as a form of execution.

Charms Objects used to bring good luck or to ward off spirits (eg rabbit's foot).

Clairaudience Hearing voices or other sounds, but not through the normal sense of hearing.

Clairsentience The ability to feel, smell or taste something without using normal senses.

Clairvoyance The ability to see things, not with the eyes, but in the 'mind's eye'.

Controls Spirits used by mediums to guide them in the spirit world, and through which mediums sometimes speak.

Cryptomnesia The ability to recall something, usually under hypnosis, not consciously remembered.

Curse An appeal to a supernatural power for harm to come to a person or group of people. Also called malediction or hex.

Demons Evil spirits which aim to harm people.

Devils Similar to demons.

Doppelgänger The ghost, or double, of the self. Also called fetch and wraith.

Dowsing The ability usually used for detecting underground water, although it can be used to detect objects and people – generally with the use of a pendulum or dowsing rod.

Ectoplasm A milky substance said to ooze from some mediums while they are in a trance.

Elementals The spirits of the four elements – air, fire, earth and water. Also spirits of nature and, sometimes, ghosts created by thought (see Tulpa).

Exorcism Ritual carried out by a clergyman to rid a person or a place of demons.

Extra-sensory perception (ESP) The ability to gain information using means other than the five senses. It includes clairvoyance, telepathy and precognition.

Familiars Demons in the form of small animals or birds, said to help witches with their spells.

Forerunner A ghostly double of the self which is seen before the real person arrives.

Funeral rites Rituals carried out at funerals to ensure that the dead rest in peace, and as a mark of respect.

Guardian spirits Ghosts and supernatural creatures who guard people against misfortune and evil spirits.

Horoscope Prediction of a person's future, based on observation of the stars and planets.

Hypnosis When a person is put in a sleep-like state, but is still able to answer questions and act on a hypnotist's suggestions.

I Ching An ancient Chinese system for obtaining advice and predicting the future.

Imitative magic Imitating the desired effect of a magical ritual using an image of the target (eg a doll to represent a person).

Legend Traditional story about an event or a person in the past, which is popularly believed, but not necessarily true.

Levitation Rising off the ground in defiance of gravity.

Ley lines Invisible lines of magnetic force, believed by some to run through the earth.

Living ghost A ghostly image of a person who is still alive, seen while the 'real' person is elsewhere.

Magic Influencing events or people through the deliberate use of spirits.

Materialize To appear suddenly in bodily form.

Medium Someone who, for some reason, can be used as a go-between, or a 'telephone line' between this world and the 'next'.

Numerology The belief that numbers have meanings and can be used to read a person's character and future.

Occult The supernatural – beyond the natural world.

Omen A sign that heralds either good or bad luck to the one who sees it.

Ouija board A board with numbers and letters through which spirits are said to communicate.

Out-of-the-body experience An experience in which the spirit (or soul) apparently leaves the body.

Palmistry Studying lines on the palms in the belief that they signify character and destiny.

Poltergeist A 'noisy ghost' often associated with children and thought to be either a manifestation of psychokinesis or a troublesome spirit.

Possession When a person is thought to have been entered and taken over by a spirit.

Precognition The ability to 'see' or know about events before they happen.

Premonition A feeling, dream, or vision about something which will happen in the future.

Prophet A person with the ability to say what will happen in the future.

Pseudopods Disembodied hands and feet produced by mediums which are either seen or felt during seances.

Psi The collective term for extra-sensory perception and psychokinesis.

Psychic Sensitivity to forces outside the natural laws of science, or someone with this sensitivity.

Psychokinesis (PK) The ability to move objects through mind power.

Radiesthesia Dowsing over a body to find the cause of an illness and its cure.

Reincarnation The rebirth of the soul, usually as another person, but sometimes as an animal or a demon.

Ritual An established practice such as a religious ceremony.

Seance A meeting led by a medium in which spirits of the dead are contacted.

Shaman Priest and magician of tribal communities.

Soul The part of a person which contains their essence, and which many believe lives on after the body dies.

Spell Words used in a special sequence to produce magic.

Spiritualism A religious movement based on the belief in life after death and the possibility of contacting the spirit world.

Subconscious A level of thoughts and memories just below the surface of the conscious mind.

Superstition A general belief in something supernatural.

Tarot cards Specially designed pack of cards used for fortune-telling.

Telepathy The ability to communicate by thought alone.

Teleportation Travelling from place to place in a short time and without visible means of transport.

Thoughtography Photographs produced by 'thinking' images onto film.

Trance A sleep-like state either self-induced or brought about by hypnosis.

Tulpa Thoughts that take on bodily form; also called mind-creatures and elementals.

Underworld The place where the souls of the dead go according to many ancient myths.

Vampire An evil spirit – or person – who can only survive by drinking the blood – or vital energy – of living creatures.

Voodoo A magic, spiritualist cult based in Haiti; called Hoodoo in parts of America.

Werebeasts Supernatural creatures which can appear in human or in animal form.

Wicca An ancient nature religion closely bound up with the idea of the earth's fertility.

Witch A person supposed to have contact with the spirit world, and be able to persuade spirits to do his or her bidding.

Witch doctor A tribal healer and spiritual leader who also sees the future and finds witches with the help of spirits.

Zener cards Specially designed cards for use in extra-sensory perception tests.

Zombies Corpses whose bodies can still function, but whose minds are dead.

ACKNOWLEDGEMENTS

The publisher has made every effort to trace ownership of all copyrighted photographs and illustrations and to secure permission for their reproduction. In the event of any question arising as to the use of such material the publisher, whilst expressing regret for inadvertent error, will be pleased to make the necessary corrections in future printings. Thanks are due to the following for permission to use the material indicated.

3   Rosalie, photo Mary Evans Picture Library
4   Freddy Jackson and his squadron
19   The Cottingley Fairies, photos Mary Evans Picture Library
25   Aleister Crowley, photo BBC Hulton Picture Library
27   Cast of hands materialized by Franek Kluski
29   Gasparetto and his paintings, photo Melvin Harris, Media Research
30   Dowsing for metals, C.16 German engraving Mary Evans Picture Library

32-33   Stanislawa Tomczyk levitating scissors, photo Mary Evans Picture Library
44   Rufus, photo top left, Colin Smythe Ltd.
     Silver Belle, photo bottom left, Topham Picture Library
44-45   Eastry Church, photo Mary Evans Picture Library
45   Ted Serios, photo bottom left, G. Brimacombe, Colorific
     Spirit photography by Ada Emma Dean, photos right, Mary Evans Picture Library

Index

William Collins Sons & Co Ltd
London · Glasgow · Sydney · Auckland
Toronto · Johannesburg

First published in Great Britain 1989
© Williams Collins Sons & Co Ltd

Printed in Great Britain by Purnell Book Production Limited
Member of the BPCC plc

Beasant, Pam
Ghosts and the supernatural.
1. Supernatural – For children
I. Title   II. Miller, Tony   III. Series
133
ISBN 0-00-190020-X
ISBN 0-00-190068-4 Pbk